Birdlight
Freeing Your Authentic Creativity

Praise for *Birdlight*

Robin Blackburn McBride demonstrates what it takes to create a vision and truly live it. She brilliantly communicates, guides, and shares what it takes to be a successful, conscious creator. *Birdlight* is unique, as Robin explores creativity through the meanings, messages, and stories of birds. This transformational book is for anyone who has a desire to create their dream project—and dream life. A highly uplifting read!
—**Peggy McColl,**
New York Times Best-Selling Author

I loved this book. As soon as I finished it (in one sitting) I wanted to re-read it and immediately dive into the exercises. Robin's disarming and intimate prose is the next best thing to having your personal life coach beside you whispering encouragement in your ear. If you are a creative person, or think you are or wish you could be, *Birdlight* will help you define your life journey with confidence.
—**Simon Choa-Johnston,**
Writer and Theatre Director, and Author of *The House of Wives*

In *Birdlight,* Robin Blackburn McBride has written an authentically raw and genuine account of the creative process. I cherish her honesty as she reflects on what a labor of love truly is—and what it takes to bring a dream to fruition. Robin takes you gently by the hand to guide you and your heart towards freedom. I feel as though I can soar in the direction of my dreams.
—**Banafsheh Akhlaghi,**
Attorney and International Best-Selling Author of
Beautiful Reminders: Anew

Robin Blackburn McBride is a passionate writer and coach who truly understands the creative process. *Birdlight* is a must-read for anyone seeking access to the immensity of their own creative power and the ability to bring it into form with grace.
—**Rodney Flowers,**
International Best-Selling Author of *Get Up!*
and *Essential Assertions*

In *Birdlight*, author Robin Blackburn McBride pulls back the curtain on the process by which creativity "works," masterfully weaving poems, folk tales, and art into her stories to simultaneously transport and transform her reader. If you're yearning for fulfillment and purpose through achievement, I highly recommend this thought-provoking and practical book.
—**Mick Petersen,**
International Best-Selling Author of *Stella and the Timekeepers*

Blessed and deeply grateful for the opportunity to read *Birdlight*, this powerful book by Robin Blackburn McBride. Robin inspires change in the lives of others as a transformational life coach, author, and speaker, and as an incredible creative and intuitive soul. These chapters are meditations and practical instructions on the creative process. As you read and work through them, you'll find that, all the more, you bring your light to the world. Robin has created a deeply meaningful book dedicated to your unique flight path. Read it, act on it, and inspire yourself forward. The world is waiting for your shining creativity!
—**Carolyn Flower,**
Owner of CFEnterprises Global and International Best-Selling Author of *Gravitate 2 Gratitude — Journal Your Journey*

Birdlight
Freeing Your Authentic Creativity

By
Robin Blackburn McBride

Copyright © 2016 Robin Blackburn McBride
All rights reserved. Published 2016

Bird sketches © 2016 Chum McLeod

This book is designed to provide information, motivation, and empowerment to readers. It is sold with the understanding that the author/publisher is not engaged to render any type of psychological, legal, or any other kind of professional advice. No warranties or guarantees are expressed or implied by the author/publisher's choice to include any of the content in this volume. Neither the publisher nor the author shall be liable for any physical, psychological, emotional, financial, or commercial damages, including, but not limited to, special, incidental, consequential, or other damages. Situations, people, and context have been changed as appropriate to protect the privacy of others.

No part of this book may be used or reproduced in any manner without written permission from the author, except in the context of reviews.

ISBN-10:0-9976215-0-8 (paperback)
ISBN-13:978-0-9976215-0-1 (paperback)
ASIN B01FSZHZJA (epub)

Book design by Profile Direct Marketing (www.allunder1roof.co).
Cover design by Patti Knoles.
Author photo by Hugh McBride.
Ebook by Efluential Publishing.

Visit Robin Blackburn McBride's website at
www.robinblackburnmcbride.com

For Charlotte

Frank Fools Crow, the great Native American holy man and healer, talked about praying each day to "become little hollow bones for the Creator's light." I love that image of emptying yourself, of becoming an instrument for beauty.
—Martha Brooks

CONTENTS

Foreword xiii

Preface xv

Introduction 1

Chapter 1
The Owl: Freeing Your Courage
    A Fairy Tale 3
    What Scares Us: Some Thoughts on Navigating Rejection 4
    Portrait of an Artist as a Young Dreamer 5
    Creation from Destruction 6
    Claiming The Owl's Gift: Courage to See in the Dark 9
    Exercise 1: The Night Visitor 10
    Exercise 2: See Your Beliefs More Clearly 12
    The Essentials So Far 14
    Key Ideas 14

Chapter 2
The Flicker: Freeing Your Trust and Confidence
    Opening the Channel 17
    Building Constructive Habits: Journal Practice 18
    Choosing to Trust Instead of Blaming 20
    Pause for Reflection: Building Trust and Confidence 22
    The Fruit of Persistence 30
    Trailing Clouds of Glory 31
    Red Feather 33
    Claiming the Flicker's Gifts: Trust and Confidence 35
    Exercise 1: Commit to a Daily Journal Practice 35
    Exercise 2: Reprogram Your Inner Playlist 35
    Exercise 3: Set a Creative Goal 37
    Key Ideas 37

Chapter 3
The Robin: Freeing Your Authenticity
    Clues to Character 39
    A Bookish Bird 40
    More Thoughts on Character and Calling 45
    An Invitation to Connect the Dots 48
    Living Authentically Now 51
    Harness the Power of Your Imagination 52
    Trust the Power of the Work Itself 54
    Creative Wellsprings: Fund Your Dream 57
    Territory 59
    Claiming the Robin's Gift: Authenticity 60
    Exercise 1: A Fond Look Back from the Future 60
    Exercise 2: Your Life Mission Statement 60
    Key Ideas 61

Chapter 4
The Crow and the Raven: Freeing Your Vision, Intuition, and Action
    One Book 63
    Black Feather 64
    The Crow: Master Caller and Collector 66
    The Call to Vision 67
    The Call to Question 69
    The Call to Commune 72
    The Call to Gather and Inspire 73
    The Call to Create: Scheduling, Planning, and Drafting 75
    The Call to Collect and Organize 76
    The Raven 80
    Key Ideas 82

Chapter 5
The Duck: Freeing Your Emotions and Discernment
    A Walk in the Sand 85
    Diving 87
    The Depths 89
    Discernment 93

    Claiming the Duck's Gift: Freeing Your Emotions and Discernment.....97
    Exercise 1: Constructive Vulnerability in the Service of Your Dream......97
    Exercise 2: Welcoming Joy 101
    Exercise 3: Soundtracking 102
    Key Ideas 103

Chapter 6
The Swan: Freeing Recognition
    Creating Your Self and Your World 105
    Dangers, Toils, and Snares 107
    Learning to See into the Life of Things 110
    Recognition: "The Ugly Duckling" 112
    Birds of a Feather 117
    Claiming The Swan's Gift:
    Recognition through Forgiveness and Revision 121
    Exercise 1: Seeing with New Eyes 121
    Exercise 2: Revision 123
    Key Ideas 125

Chapter 7
The Eagle: Freeing Your Ability to Soar
    The Gift of Expectation 127
    The Eagle 131
    Quantum Leaping 136
    Detachment 138
    Claiming the Eagle's Gift: Soaring with Perspective 140
    Exercise 1: Raise Your Altitude through Study 140
    Exercise 2: Raise Your Strength through Listening 141
    Exercise 3: Explore Guided Imagery for Motivation 141
    Key Ideas 146

Postscript 148
Acknowledgments 149
Bibliography 151
Meet Robin Blackburn McBride 156
My Heartfelt Wish for You 158

Foreword

Congratulations. You've made a great decision to read Robin Blackburn McBride's book on creativity and take action for your dream. Robin's work is rich in inspiration and valuable strategies for moving forward in your life and on your creative path. Here you'll find practical steps you can take right away to live your life from a place of greater clarity, purpose, authenticity, and conscious creativity—joyfully!

While Robin calls me her mentor, I call her my friend. And what I know is that she brings natural artistry to her words and to her life. Robin is a gifted writer and coach. Based on my forty-plus years of studying, codifying, and teaching a system of dream building that absolutely works—and my experience training coaches who are at the forefront of the personal development field—I can tell you Robin is someone you can absolutely count on to be a transformer in your life.

My success came from applying the learning I gained from turning to people who were successful at doing the things I wanted to do. Robin has studied and applied her learning for many years and she has real gifts for you—not only in her creative abilities, but in the conscious choice she makes each day to deepen her understanding and application of success principles for the benefit of others. She is a Master Teacher.

Robin works in the lineage of dream builders. She lays bare the key turning points from her past: moments which at first glance appeared as adversity, and which have yielded far greater benefits than she initially imagined. She is vulnerable and real for *you*, so that you may recognize the creative potential in ALL of your experience and grow.

Throughout this book are many personal anecdotes, lessons, and recommended exercises, as well as excerpts from theater, poetry, folk and fairy tales, and works by other thought leaders and artists. The creative *weave* of this inspired text is distinctive—a book of teaching stories, luminous passages, explorations in artistry, and highly charged calls to action.

Robin has a compelling way of imparting the lessons she's learned, and these lessons will give you everything you're looking for to begin transforming your life. Look for mysterious and beautiful occurrences to show up as you read this book and say a resounding *yes*, each day, to your dream.

Study this book. Invest in yourself by working with Robin at every opportunity, and let your heart and your life soar. You deserve to create your life by design and bring your authentic contributions and artistry into form. You deserve to live a life you truly LOVE living.

I will be sharing with Robin the gifts I've gained from this amazing book.

I hope you do too!

Mary Morrissey
Simi Valley, California, 2016

Preface

Creativity is by no means exclusive to artists or those engaged in any particular pursuit, practice, or field of innovation. It's our birthright. There is no such thing as an "uncreative" person.

The life we've each been given has the potential to be the greatest work of art we will ever realize. In that spirit, as you read *Birdlight*, I invite you to read "art" and "artist" in any way that feels personally relevant to you.

At first glance, this book may appear to be directed primarily to people with conventionally artistic inclinations; undoubtedly, early in its conception I invited connection with others seeking a return to passion through the arts. With that said, the clients I have the privilege of serving come from all walks of life. In fact, at present, the majority of people who attend my talks and workshops, and those who coach with me in groups and privately, are not artists in any traditional sense. They all, however, share in a sense of the vastness of their own creative potential. They are drawn by a deep inner wisdom to unblock the creative wellspring that is theirs by nature, and are called to direct their efforts consciously in this world, aligned with their true character and sense of mission.

The results are often both amazing and moving.

I am profoundly thankful in the depth and scope of our work together, which continues to expand and inform my life.

Robin Blackburn McBride
Toronto, Canada, 2016

Introduction

Birds are nature's emblems of creative freedom and vision. We delight in watching their ease of motion, including the ability to soar. I didn't set out to organize this book by birds; in fact, I didn't see the book coming at all. In a midwinter moment of disappointment and questioning, birds found me. Then this book came. Not when I railed at life's letdowns, or at the story of my shortcomings, or at the fear that my choices over the past year, indeed, my life, had been misguided. No. It found me when I sat down quietly and lit a candle.

In calm and humility came restoration, renewed confidence, and rededication. A prayer and firelight brought wings.

One of the most powerful ideas I've come across in many years of studying creativity, learning to trust an artistic calling and developing a writing practice, is the belief that what we yearn for also yearns for us. You may have discovered this book because of a deep longing to live more creatively—that is, to create by *design* rather than by default. If you take nothing else away, please take this potentially transformative thought: Know the life you desire is actually calling you; it longs for you as much as you long for it. Your love and longing are requited. Your life of creative fulfillment waits for you to take the actions necessary to realize it, regardless of your age and present circumstance.

For twenty years I worked in education, which taught me much and gave me countless gifts, including the gift of joy, yet part of me pined for more time to write. On his door, one of my colleagues once posted this quote, attributed to Oliver Wendell Holmes: "Many people die with their music still in them. Why is this so? Too often it is because they are always getting ready to live. Before they know it, time runs out." Reading that message, I felt frustrated, even ashamed, at all the reasons why much of my "music," as yet unwritten, was still locked away inside. I felt I wasn't fully living the life I was meant to live, and that it was my fault for failing to make it happen.

If your experience has been similar, if you feel your music—or whatever your creative calling is—locked deep inside and somehow inaccessible to you, know that you are not alone. Many people who appear to be highly functional and satisfied, even gifted and prosperous in their work, yearn for transformation. Yet stronger than their yearning is their fear—and they allow that fear to hold them back. This book of stories and practical exercises is designed to help you build a creative life where dreams triumph over fears.

I hope that as you read, each bird calls to you in a way that resonates with your particular journey and mission. I wish you creative confidence and freedom, and the power to bring your music, whatever it may be, into form—as only *you* can.

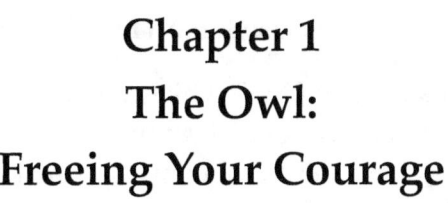

Chapter 1
The Owl:
Freeing Your Courage

What you seek is seeking you.
—Rumi

A Fairy Tale

"The Owl," a little-known, yet in some ways all-too-familiar, Grimm brothers tale begins with "one of the great owls" from the woods seeking haven in a local townsman's barn. At dawn, the owl doesn't leave her newfound perch. The servant who first sets eyes on her is so alarmed that he announces a monster has arrived in the community, and news of the great horned visitor soon wreaks havoc on the town. Townsperson after townsperson, each bearing arms, attempts to slay "the strange, grim creature," only to flee the barn in terror. Eventually, even the mightiest warrior loses his nerve at the sight of the secretly bewildered animal as she resorts to rolling her eyes (presumably the third eyelids that owls have), ruffling her feathers, flapping her wings, harshly snapping her beak and crying "tuwhit, tuwhoo"—at which the warrior nearly faints, falling back to the rallying crowd. The townsfolk then accuse the monster of poisoning and mortally wounding the very strongest of men among them. "So," the tale concludes, "they set fire to the barn at all four corners, and with it the owl was miserably burnt."

Of course, the story's ending is both credible and eerily predictable. The owl, long associated with wisdom, intuition, magic, and vision, is a target from the start, its large presence perceived as both startling and strange. Each witness views the creature as a threat, and each agrees with the unsettling being's destruction.

What Scares Us: Some Thoughts on Navigating Rejection

I read "The Owl" while researching my second novel, on the heels of receiving several publishers' rejections of my first. Bewildered, I was tempted to view my spurned manuscript like that unwelcome bird—a doomed creation, too strange and grim for a major house to take a risk on. Over the years of visioning, researching, writing, and revising that novel, I had found reason to believe in its worth—not just to me, but to others. Several readers, including an established novelist, a teacher, and a prominent literary agent, had rallied behind my work. Buoyed by their support and guided by my own strong intuition, I had taken the risk of leaving a twenty-year teaching career and leapt faithfully to the rafters of a new life. Over five months, I had reworked the novel with an editor. I'd invested time in taking my historical research further, and consulted an addiction specialist to verify the realism of my protagonist's interior life—something I'd worked hard to establish. After the agent read my revised copy, she praised the work (which meant a lot, coming from someone who does *not* readily pay compliments), and I (ha, ha) visualized an immediate sale. When rejection e-mails followed, it took strength and mental conditioning not to see them as swords and flames.

If I read "The Owl" as a metaphor for my novel (or, worse, for me)—a victim of external forces—I knew the bird had no hope of flying. At times I began to doubt my work, replaying critics' words in my mind. It was tempting to leave the file in the drawer.

What happens when a sensitive and committed creative person experiences rejection? And why begin a book on unblocking, developing, and trusting creativity with such a story? Of course, the answers to the first question will vary widely, depending on who is being asked. In this chapter, I'll show you the answers of two people—the young and vulnerable person I once was and the more consciously focused and resilient person I became—in order to illustrate two very different possibilities. In so doing, I hope to show the reason for beginning what seeks to be an uplifting and motivational book with a barn burning.

Portrait of an Artist as a Young Dreamer

When I was a child and a young woman, bold, impractical, and passionate, I felt a clear call to live this lifetime as an artist. Growing up, I experienced a strong pull to creative expression through a variety of modes, including writing, acting, visual art, music, and dance. When my parents drew the line at buying me dance lessons, I bought them myself with babysitting and summer job money. I wrote stories and delivered speeches throughout junior and middle school, earned lead roles in plays from elementary days to university, and won performance awards at grade school and college. I completed my first degree in drama and set out for a life in theater. But when it came to fielding rejections, I was a complete novice—uninitiated, uneducated, and dangerously vulnerable. Very little existed in the way of personal development books in the eighties, and so I relied on fate, not faith, hoping desperately to be "discovered," while with every rejection my confidence shrank. I became self-conscious and disconnected from my audition performances, which suddenly felt humiliating. My apparent boldness, carried over from my student days, became empty, embarrassing. While still earnest in my desire to heed the artist's call, for the first time, I doubted my own inner voice. Often, I couldn't hear it at all. I became the opposite of the successful self I had been as a student performer. While I made it into several professional shows, each felt more like a life raft than an affirmation. Ultimately, an inexperienced acting teacher's unkind words, spoken rashly in a moment of unchecked anger, were enough to send me out the door.

Instead of surrounding myself with a supportive team and learning how to use the constructive power of my thoughts, I did what many young people do: I abandoned my own artistic aspirations and fell in love with a performing artist instead. To be clear, I don't mean to minimize the value and importance of that significant chapter in my life, which lasted for many years. While the marriage eventually came to an end, it led to growth and yielded gifts, the greatest of all being a daughter who is now a wonderful woman. I look back in gratitude for the unexpected offerings that life's challenges and sudden turns often bring.

Nonetheless....

When I was very young I knew I was artistically inclined, but I didn't recognize and trust my own ability to access the inner strength and vision necessary to create the life I truly desired. I didn't realize that what was inside of me, indeed inside all of us—for I am certainly no exception—was far bigger and greater than any present circumstance. So I gave up on my career plan. Furthermore, I blamed myself for abandoning the life I'd dreamed of.

At this point, I trust that you find at least some of my story is familiar. Have you experienced moments of self-sabotage and, perhaps, the loss of a dream? Have your creative self-image and confidence ever taken a beating? Have you been constricted in your creative life and felt quietly (or not so quietly) desperate to find your path when it seemed like you were on the wrong one?

I expect you have, because while each of us is unique, this story is very common.

> You enter the forest
> at the darkest point,
> where there is no path.

The dark forest is the owl's true home. At the beginning of the Grimm brothers' tale, the owl arrives from the neighboring wood: an unknown place, a place of opportunities, and a place we also fear. An initiatory animal, the owl sometimes portends a death. Certainly it sees in the dark.

Creation from Destruction

In watching my dream die, I was at least able to see new possibilities. I chose a career that matched my skill set, one that felt safe and offered meaning. At home one night with my little baby, I decided to embark on the path to becoming a teacher—a profession which my brother still affectionately refers to as "the family business." I had been raised by teachers and certainly knew something of the territory. The fit was natural enough and caused everyone in my life to sigh with relief. For me, secretly, the best part was that in order to earn my teaching degree I'd have to return to university and specialize in English. I found my passion again, and for two glorious years I took care of my baby by day while by night I studied the tomes of literary luminaries, often staying up until 2:00 or 3:00 a.m. writing essays and poetry.

Ironically, while I did everything I could to ensure my acceptance to the Faculty of Education, secretly I hoped for rejection this time. If it came, I was prepared to take the opportunity instead to go to graduate school, where I could continue studying literature. Yet the doors of the teachers college did open to me. I studied, and upon graduation I immediately earned a teaching position.

I could write a book on the many gifts of teaching school for twenty years, but it would not be this book.

This book is for you.

Did you ever reach a point at which you knew the following lines to be true?

> Where there is a way or path,
> it is someone else's path.
>
> You are not on your own path.

As wonderful as it was to teach in an outstanding school environment, with its beautiful community, constructive challenges, ongoing learning, joys, and advantages, it didn't call to me in the way that old deep, authentic voice inside still did. Many days, I wished that institutional teaching *had* called me from within, and loudly, too—then my life would have been so much more straightforward. I wouldn't have spent so many summer holidays scribbling down poems and stories, seeing my first poetry book published in my "spare time," walking ravines with a notebook, researching historical settings at the library in July, mapping plots and scratching things out only to begin again, writing a novel. I could have relaxed like a "normal person"—though I sincerely had no idea what that would look like for me. I knew that many of my colleagues were doing powerful, profound work, living in alignment with a sacred call, but I also knew their call was different from mine.

Eventually, when I'd learned how to fully reclaim my own creative life—when I had written enough and built enough strength and resources to withstand whatever came my way and to live fully, deliberately, I decided to go home to the woods.

> You enter the forest
> at the darkest point,
> where there is no path.
>
> Where there is a way or path,
> it is someone else's path.
>
> You are not on your own path.
>
> If you follow someone else's way,
> you are not going to realize
> your potential.
>
> —Joseph Campbell

Needless to say, at age forty-eight, when I received the editors' rejection e-mails, I didn't fold. This book is, in part, intended to show you how to remain strong when the going gets rough. But it is more: it is also about how to heed your creative calling. To do that, you must have courage.

What struck me in reading "The Owl" so soon after withstanding rejection was how important it is to recognize that there is not only a magical and sacred voice inside each of us, but also the voices of the terrified townsfolk. We are our own harshest critics. The only truly powerful rejection is that which comes from within. External circumstances merely reflect what's on our minds.

The greatest challenge, beyond having courage, is having compassion for the small self in struggling to unite with the higher self—recognizing that fear of death and humiliation (for some, equally weighted) is what the townsfolk experience in the great owl's presence. And fear is as natural as the forest. If you can learn to live with fear and uncertainty, then you can live with the magical owl. And you will never look back.

Claiming The Owl's Gift:
Courage to See in the Dark

You'll need a journal and a fast-writing pen for the exercises in this book. I recommend that you complete the first assignment within a week's time, and that you hold off on reading further until you've finished your "meeting with the night visitor" in the exercise that follows. If you're eager to keep reading, then meet tonight! Work through this book at a pace that's right for you.

Not by accident, you begin with an assignment that has the potential to scare you, or, at the very least, put you off. Resistance is natural; every one of us experiences it, and what initially registers as boredom or edginess often signals a deeper fear. Our fear and resistance point us directly to our gifts. They stand at the doorway to our personal gold: unrealized potential. Noticing our own resistance is empowering, because by watching it we have the opportunity to overcome it and make real progress. In case you're thinking "This is fine for some people, but I don't need to bother" or "I've already done this sort of thing before" or "I just want to see where she's going," remember that your purpose in reading this book is to see where *you* are going. In order to set your own course, you must become skilled at following through on plans. Presumably, you have planned to complete this book. Each time you overcome resistance along the way, mark it down as a win. And if you don't feel like doing an exercise, it's especially important that you do it. Start now. Give yourself that win for following through.

Exercise 1: The Night Visitor

Prepare a private space at your home for solo time out. This is an opportunity to deeply relax, without sleeping. It's important that you remain awake for this visioning exercise. This is a night journey. Choose an evening when your work is complete and you are guaranteed privacy. You may wish to dim the lights and sit by a candle; owls are famous for being able to see in the dark. Close the door. If you listen to music, choose something instrumental, preferably percussive and low. When you relax with quiet music, you engage the right brain, conducive to visioning.

Have a journal with pre-written questions handy as prompts. Over time, you'll become good at asking your own questions; for your first try at this exercise, use the prompts given below.

Take a few minutes just to settle into your chair, or onto a meditation cushion. Your imagination is a hugely powerful mental faculty. Use it now, recalling Albert Einstein's famous line "Imagination is more important than knowledge." I invite you to believe or imagine that a clear and direct connection with a creative source is occurring; think of that source any way you like: your higher self or higher power, God, a divine presence, the quantum field, your creative spirit, the universe, etc.

Respond to the questions below, writing quickly. Allow ideas to flow from your pen without judgment. Don't censor.

In your imagination, welcome the arrival of an animal. You have just read about the owl, and you may wish to welcome that bird in your mind. If you do, consider that there are many types. The presence of a charming barred owl will be very different from that of a great horned owl, and a majestic, patient snowy owl differs significantly from a screech owl. You may wish to read up on owl varieties in a book, such as Ted Andrews' *Animal Speak*. You may wish to work with a different animal altogether, perhaps a mammal or a reptile. If you like, allow yourself to be surprised by the creature that enters your mental picture.

Whatever visitor arrives, invite it to stay with you for this core journaling practice. And do call it that—practice. There are no mistakes in this activity, and you can always repeat it. For now, as you relax and sit, simply feel what it's like to be in the presence of this nocturnal visitor. Feel the creature's specific strengths, its gifts. Allow sensations to come. Know that if you choose to do this exercise again, other gifts will reveal themselves—all have meaning, all have import in your creative journey. The visits are guideposts.

Consider your magic animal to be the embodiment of your creativity, your own personal magic. Even if you don't believe it, pretend to. Allow yourself to play.

Questions
Ask the following questions of your visitor.

1. **What are you here to show me about my creativity?** Allow for any answer. It could be in the form of words—a sentence or a whole paragraph. It could be an image that flashes before your mind's eye. It could be a sound in your mind. Ask repeatedly, allowing for more information to come each time. Write down all the information you receive, without stopping. Don't judge. No one else sees your notes.

2. **In what ways are you strong and beautiful?** Again, just allow. If something comes up that you reject, allow it anyway. It's very important just to flow it out.

3. **What about you do I fear?** Be prepared to go big here. Let the

worst thoughts come, recognizing them as just that: thoughts.

4. **Why is it important for me to heed your call?** Dig deep. You know it's important or you wouldn't be doing this.

5. **What actions can I take within my existing life structure to allow your wisdom and presence?** Sit with this question as long as you need to and don't judge what comes. Let the ideas flow, as crazy or threatening or wonderful as they seem. Just let them take form in your mind and on the page.

After you've completed the exercise, don't reread your notes. Instead, take a few minutes to reflect on the experience you've just had. Give thanks to your creative source for being so clearly present. Accept with gratitude whatever insight you've gained, even if it's come through discomfort, doubt, and resistance. If you like, write about the experience—but again, don't reread what you've written yet. Simply be with the notes and your thoughts, in gratitude.

Schedule some early-morning time the next day, or the day after that, to read over your notes. Reread them again in a week's time, and then again in a month. You may be surprised at what you discover. Whatever happens, don't judge yourself or fear any aspect of your vision and follow-up writing. Simply set an intention for constructive, positive learning to come from the experience. If anything happens that isn't comfortable for you, lean in and ask to be shown its positive, constructive meaning.

You may wish to repeat the exercise, perhaps modifying it—or you may feel you've learned what you needed.

Exercise 2: Seeing Your Beliefs More Clearly

After you have read and reflected on your notes from "The Night Visitor," dedicate two pages in your journal to listing ideas under these titles: "My Empowering Beliefs about My Creativity" and "My Disempowering Beliefs about My Creativity." When you list your disempowering thoughts, the point is not to beat yourself up for recognizing negativity within yourself, but just the opposite: to acknowledge your courage in becoming aware of the old learned messages which have been shaping the experiences you create.

Our learned beliefs have a huge impact on our reality. When we change underlying negative thought patterns, we change our reality—but that can only happen when we're willing to (a) recognize the paradigm (the set of old beliefs, thoughts, and habits) we've been operating from and (b) do what it takes to realign our beliefs with who we truly are. Soon, I'll offer ways to do that. For now, take heart in having made a good start.

Reward yourself for being courageous in looking honestly at your beliefs, both positive and negative. Pay attention to your feelings. Regardless of what they are, mark the occasion by giving yourself a win for taking a risk. Choosing to view an act of risk-taking—of pushing through resistance—as a win increases the amount of the chemical messenger dopamine in the brain. In his ground-breaking book *The Winner Effect*, neuropsychologist Ian Robertson emphasizes that acknowledging our successes, even small ones, is a key determinant of subsequent experiences: "Dopamine makes us smarter and more bold." He advises, "Contrive small successes to get big successes." In his famous 2012 TED Talk, "How to Build Your Creative Confidence," design visionary David Kelley echoes that advice by drawing a connection between experiencing "a series of small successes" and developing greater creativity, resilience, perseverance and self-efficacy—"the sense that you can change the world and that you can attain what you set out to do."

Give yourself a win for your success in completing the Chapter 1 exercises. Seal your success by making a statement of commitment in your journal to live creatively and to play full out. You choose your own words and the length. Here is an example:

> I, _____, commit to building my confidence and freeing my creativity with vision, courage, passion, and meaning.

My successful creative work has profound and positive gifts, not only for me but for others—indeed, most especially for others.
I AM ALREADY THE PERSON I DREAM OF BEING.

Sign and date your commitment.

> The moment you commit and quit holding back, all sorts of unforeseen incidents, meetings and material assistance, will rise up to help you. The simple act of commitment is a powerful magnet for help.
> —Napoleon Hill

The Essentials So Far

Choose three to five of the following key ideas from this chapter and write them on large cards. Where appropriate, change "you" to "I," etc. to make the statements your own. Post the messages where you will read and reread them daily. Only post the ideas which *you* find most relevant and important right now. If wall space isn't available for posting them, then make the messages into wallpaper for your computer, or put them in your Outlook or Google calendar so they'll pop up as reminders. Or write them on cards that only you will see and carry them in your wallet. You can make new cards any time. If you like, do this exercise at the end of every chapter.

Key Ideas

- The creative call itself is proof of its importance. The life you desire longs for you as much as you long for it.
- Give yourself a win each time you overcome a fear and push through resistance to do what's important to you.
- Creativity is natural and spiritual and one with all experience.
- Constructive thinking skills are just as important—at times even more important—than the skills of one's particular craft.

Conscious thought power is the key to surmounting obstacles on the creative path.

- Listen to that deep, ageless, and authentic inner voice that calls you to create.
- The only truly powerful rejection is that which comes from within.
- You can choose to accept your call, your gifts, and your human imperfections with compassion and a sincere, daily commitment to grow.
- The mind can be reconditioned to create consciously from positive thoughts rather than negative ones.
- Notice your thoughts and emotional reactions. Become aware of your resistance, with a view to developing creative strength and mastery.
- Schedule time for quiet solitude—often. Create conditions for cultivating intuition and imagination.
- Actively engage your imagination, for it "embraces the entire world and all there will ever be to know and understand" (Einstein).
- Acknowledge your courage in becoming more aware of your own learned set of core messages, and in becoming willing to change the attitudes and beliefs that no longer serve you creatively.
- Reward yourself for even small successes. Develop a winner's mind-set.
- Your creativity is ageless.
- Commit to realizing your creative dreams. Imagine and *feel* that you are already living the life of your dreams.

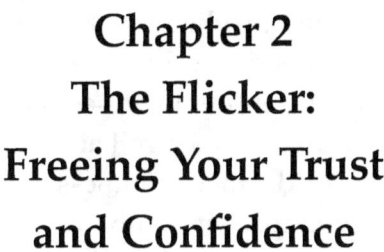

Chapter 2
The Flicker:
Freeing Your Trust
and Confidence

You can't get to your dream; you must come from it. —Mary Morrissey

Opening the Channel

Magic happened when I stepped outside and found the March sun warm enough to free me from my coat. We'd been buried in snow all winter in Toronto. But now, even though the dirty-white domes of old snowbanks still towered, their crusty surfaces glistened with meltwater. I threw salt at the base of the garage door which had stuck days earlier and, as I did, felt brilliantly buoyed by my boys'-size-six rubber boots. Open sesame! The child in me knew my next mission: shovel a path to the deck, where I'd not stood in months. My rubber toes poked happily at the drifts. Elated, I started digging. I scaled the deck and liberated the patio cushions which had been stuck to the chairs, half-buried, for ages. How well I could relate.

Shoveling was a welcome break from sitting in my office, and one which allowed me the joy of single-pointed focus. Our minds are often pulled in different directions when we sit at our desks, yet not when we are doing a simple, physical task. As I beheld the winter dirt, the withered plants and stray wrappers, the unidentified, once-flying, tiny plastic objects, and the neighbors' cigarette butts, I gave my attention entirely to clearing debris. I didn't think about the hours of work on projects waiting indoors. All I wanted was to shovel, sweep, and wipe away winter. My actions found a rhythm, and I didn't feel like I was working. I felt glorious. Suddenly, ideas for my second novel flooded my mind—another unexpected open sesame! An entire novel sequence flowed through this channel as I became aware of a familiar sound. Sure enough, when I looked up I discovered a merry witness to my pleasure: a flicker. This member of the woodpecker family was a welcome sight—and a colorful synchronicity—perched high in a Chinese elm tree.

One of the projects on my desk was the upcoming section on journaling, or "mark making" as I think of it. The bird I'd long associated with journaling was none other than the woodpecker, a creature that derives nourishment from the trees it marks. Several boughs of the elm had splintered off in a December ice storm. On one level, the tree was ugly now, broken and seemingly ruined. But for the flicker, the tree was a great source of life. Woodpeckers know the best insects are often found inside dead branches. We can learn from these birds that use even brokenness to thrive: we, too, can use every experience as a channel for creative nourishment.

When I came inside to a hot cup of coffee with my new novel sequence in my head, feeling a rush of delight from the fresh air and bird sighting, I reflected on just how little I had traded for such gifts—the simple effort to go out and move some snow.

Then I reached for my journal.

Building Constructive Habits: Journal Practice

Journal writing is a simple, focused activity. It requires only single-pointed attention and the willingness to write freely. The physical act of pen-to-paper journaling becomes rhythmic when we allow ourselves to channel the messages that want to emerge. As soon as we judge our words and thoughts, fluidity and rhythm stop. Channeling language while suspending judgment is a key to finding flow and, ultimately, meaning. Years ago, I'd had an art teacher who used the term "mark making" in place of "drawing." This substitution helped her students overcome their fear of making mistakes—how can you make mistakes if you're simply making marks? Another art teacher told me that in order to get anywhere as an artist, a person has to use a lot of paper. She didn't say "to waste" paper, but "to use" it—and freely! Nothing is a waste if we use it; that includes every experience of our lives. Journaling helps us to use everything. When we allow ourselves to write on a daily basis, regardless of our jobs, assignments, or chores, and no matter what our preferred modes of creative expression are, we make space for setting down the experiences and ideas that want to be seen. We connect with our own inner guidance. We relax. Thoughts flow freely. We cultivate awareness. We reflect. The more honest and uninhibited we are, the more rhythmic, intuitive, and fruitful the process becomes.

I make the connection between journal writing and the flicker quite naturally, because the industrious woodpecker links the observer to the rhythms of the world—the same world we can listen to and read for its messages. In setting the world down on the page, we see it more deeply. In *Animal Speak*, Ted Andrews writes that the flicker reminds us to "peck away at deception until truth is revealed." Consider all the ways we deceive ourselves when we merely skim the surface of experience. We can so easily jump to conclusions, judging rashly and living our lives in reactive, reductive jot-notes, hurtling through a world of Internet searches, social media, e-mail, news, ringing telephones, transit rides, deadlines, television, video games, and the like. We live in a culture of sound bites. Yet the mind is our most powerful tool. To cultivate awareness, to use the mind for honest expression and reflection, for discernment and clear intention, is to employ our most valuable "technology." The practice of journaling daily shows us what's on our minds. Without reflective time, without the freedom to set down experiences, to see where the mind leads on the page, to witness even our own noticing, there is little opportunity for finding depth and stillness. Andrews writes that the flicker's drumming "is a reminder of the natural rhythms of the universe and that when we are not in synchronicity with them, things do not work for us." Making room for daily journaling invites a life wherein things *do* work for us.

As my favorite tea-bag tag reminds me, "A relaxed mind is a creative mind." In the language of neuroscience, such a mind is one which habitually engages the prefrontal cortex — that is, a mind conditioned to pause and reroute the processing of experience from the deeply embedded, primal "lizard brain" (the almond-sized, emotionally reactive, amygdala) to the frontal lobe area associated with calm and choice, and an experience of balance. Finding balance in daily experience is necessary for relaxation. Again the flicker serves as a reminder to live wisely. Its feet are unusual in the bird world; they're designed to give the animal balance, regardless of conditions, as it negotiates tree trunks. Daily self-expression, giving oneself permission to channel whatever comes to mind directly onto the page, is a way of inviting balance, meaning, relaxation and conscious creativity into one's life.

Choosing to Trust Instead of Blaming

For the artistic soul, regardless of occupation, age, or stage of development, consciously inviting creativity into daily experience is essential to well-being. Yet so often, naturally innovative, expressive people find themselves out of balance, cut off from the peace of creative flow. They blame external conditions for a sense of loss, and feel the pain of abandoning their gifts acutely. I write from personal experience — for years I blamed my own choices for separating me from a sense of fulfillment. I blamed the need to survive, to please, and to be a provider. I blamed an overly full schedule for robbing me of a life I felt intuitively drawn to and blocked from at the same time; I didn't know how to transcend the paradox. It took years for me to understand that by crowding out daily creative expression, putting it last on my priority list instead of first, I was actually abandoning a core part of myself, sabotaging my trust in life. The only way to trust again was to make creative expression and personal development time my first priority of the day.

When I began putting journal writing first, getting up earlier to make it happen, my whole life changed. While some of the initial effects of that shift were disruptive and even painful at the time, all were liberating and eventually brought the joy of consciously creating new pathways. The shift itself was growth; certainly it was better and healthier than staying stuck.

Committing to daily journal writing is an ongoing act of trust. It helps build what pioneering success author Napoleon Hill calls "habitforce." It contributes to the development of self-reliance, something Hill claims is necessary for the persistence required to achieve creative goals. Journaling is also meditative, emotionally demanding, and humbling. In her famous manifesto for writers, *Writing Down the Bones*, Natalie Goldberg compares daily writing with Zen Buddhist practice; she honors the beginner's mind as "what we must come back to every time we sit down and write." Being beginners, we remain fresh—and also vulnerable. Allowing ourselves to be constructively vulnerable, to take emotional risks for the sake of growth, is crucial not only to being an artist of any kind, but to being open to experiencing beauty and connection. In her book *One Continuous Mistake: Four Noble Truths for Writers*, author Gail Sher also likens writing to Zen practice. The last of her "noble truths" is my favorite, because it redefines failure in the context of creative expression: "If writing is your practice, the only way to fail is not to write." So often, people fear making marks on paper because they fear being judged for the quality of their output. But if failing is simply not doing the thing you want to do, fear of failure is easily overcome. One of my most instructive and inspirational creativity teachers has been Julia Cameron, who urges artists simply to "show up at the page."

Simple is good, but not always easy. It requires discipline. Building trust can be simple if one commits to a daily creative practice, and trust is a crucial key—one which ultimately builds confidence.

Pause for Reflection: Building Trust and Confidence

Free-flowing daily journaling is an awareness practice, and one of several daily routines I recommend for tapping into your immense creative power. The more you can count on yourself to invest time each day in personal development practices, the more you build self-trust and creative confidence.

In the reflective quiz below, I invite you to think about your habits and your level of creative self-trust. Do your best to consider each question carefully and to highlight the appropriate answer. Look for a pattern, not a score. The letters aren't grades; they represent a continuum. This activity is not about self-judgment, only honest introspection. Your answers can't be measured quantitatively. Only *you* can determine the messages of greatest value to you here.

1. **How much time do you commit, on a daily basis, to journaling?**
    a) *I don't have a journal practice of any kind. I've just been too busy.*
    b) *I have a journal, but I hesitate to write in it. I'm afraid that my writing will ruin it, and that others might read it. I'd like to get past these fears.*
    c) *2–10 minutes, occasionally. I usually only do it when I'm inspired.*
    d) *11–20 minutes. I write in a journal most days, when I have a chance.*
    e) *20–30 minutes daily, usually at about the same time(s) each day.*
    f) *30–60 minutes or more daily, at the same time(s) each day, at least five days a week.*

2. **To what extent do you give yourself credit for simply "showing up" to write in your journal and for building resilience? Do you give yourself regular wins?**
    a) *None, because I don't have a journal practice. Thinking about "wins" for simply doing something, regardless of quality, elicits my cynicism.*

I think about all the "participation prizes" in school that seemed so bogus.

b) *Rarely. On the odd occasion when I've written in a journal, I haven't usually seen merely "showing up" as valuable. Once or twice, maybe.*

c) *Only occasionally, and then usually only because I've written something I like.*

d) *Sometimes I credit myself for showing up. I don't want to judge the quality of my journal writing, although often I can't help it.*

e) *I usually feel good about my journal writing because I know that devoting time to reflection is worthwhile. With that said, I don't always think to give myself a win.*

f) *I consistently give myself daily wins for showing up. I know I can give myself a command and follow it, and I earn wins for consistent efforts, unattached to product quality.*

3. **Consider the words of early self-help author Wallace Wattles: "Gratitude will lead your mind out along the ways by which things come; and it will keep you in close harmony with creative thought and prevent you from falling into competitive thought." How often do you pause and reflect in gratitude for your journal practice, which helps you to cultivate an awareness of your honest thoughts and feelings? Are you ever grateful for any other creative experiences? (Remember to select and honor the answer below that's closest to being accurate for you. Don't judge it.)**

a) *I don't have a journal practice to be grateful for, and so far, I've never thought to be grateful for my few-and-far-between creative experiences.*

b) *I hear a lot about the importance of being grateful, and I wish I could be, but I find it hard. Very occasionally I feel grateful for a creative achievement, although most of the time, I'm more likely to feel dissatisfied. It's my nature to be self-critical.*

c) *Occasionally I feel grateful for my creative experiences. Usually the feeling is attached to achievement. So far, I've never felt grateful just for showing up to write in a journal; I have to accomplish something impressive in order to be grateful for it.*

d) *Sometimes I feel grateful for my journal practice. The temptation is to attach gratitude only to achievement; I occasionally take a moment to feel grateful for simply showing up.*

e) *I often feel grateful for my journal practice experiences of self-awareness. I understand that feeling gratitude helps me to attract more creatively beneficial experiences. I don't always remember to pause and list what I'm grateful for, and I'd like to make more efforts to do that.*

f) *I make a habit of pausing during each of my daily journal sessions and taking stock of several things I'm grateful for in that moment, including the practice itself. I've learned that routine gratitude checks are uplifting. They tend to invite more experiences to celebrate and be grateful for, not the least of which is my creative work.*

4. **To what extent does your journal practice contribute to your creative well-being? For example, does it connect with your larger creative goals? Does it give you insight into your own creative process and growth? Does it contribute to feelings of peace, ease, and balance, which make creativity welcome?**

a) *I have no journal or other daily practice of pausing to reflect and become deeply aware of what I'm thinking and feeling; therefore, I make no connection.*

b) *I don't have a journal practice, but occasionally I wish I did. I'd like to develop the self-discipline to write intuitively every day and see where the experiment leads.*

c) *Because my journal practice is sporadic, up until now my awareness of its importance has been minimal. Occasionally I jot something down that makes sense, and it gives me clarity on an issue, or new ideas — even creative ones. I'd like to do more of this.*

d) *Sometimes my journal leads me to think of ideas for new creative ventures, and sometimes I gain insights into my experience, desires, and sense of mission. I'd like to learn how to deepen my journal experience so that it feels more relevant and integrated into my creative evolution.*

e) *I often make connections between my journal practice and my well-being. Sometimes my practice includes reflecting on my growth through challenging experiences. Sometimes I notice how calm and glad I feel to have time to myself, in silence each day, for a practice unattached to outcomes. Sometimes while writing in my journal I experience flashes of insight that contribute to my creative projects.*

f) *I've come to expect magic in my ordinary experience of journal writing. The journal is my conduit to meaning, inspiration, and practical next steps. It's a place where I see what I say, and grow.*

5. **What is the level of connection between your intuition and your creative process?**

a) *I don't feel intuitive and don't sense a connection.*

b) *My intuition feels minimal to me at this point, and therefore any connection is also minimal.*

c) *Occasionally I have an intuitive flash that connects me with my creative process.*

d) *Sometimes I find that my journal writing leads to intuitive insights and synchronicities in my daily experience. I'd like to incorporate more of this experience in my creative process beyond the journal.*

e) *Often my intuition engages as I work and live creatively. Reflections in my journal are a seedbed for further intuitive, creative experiences.*

f) *My intuition is strong, and it contributes both to my creative process and to my confidence daily.*

6. **Up until now, to what extent have you trusted yourself to set creative goals and to follow through on achieving them?**

a) *Not at all. I feel self-doubt and reluctance in this area.*

b) *Rarely have I felt I could count on myself to set and follow through on a creative goal — that is, beyond the parameters of my paid work and family life. I'd like to trust myself to set substantial, far-reaching, and authentic creative goals, and to see them through to completion. So far, I haven't set very specific goals.*

c) *Occasionally I've set creative goals, but then I've doubted I could achieve them. In the past, my goals were either vague or unrealistic and daunting. I've allowed myself to dream a little — sometimes a lot — but up until now, my dreaming has often led to a sense of yearning and frustration. I'd like to improve my creative self-trust.*

d) *Sometimes I've had the experience of setting a creative goal and seeing it through all or most of the way. With that said, in the past, my lack of confidence has hindered me in building upon those experiences. I'd love to get beyond self-doubt, to set greater goals and to thrive creatively.*

e) *I've been fortunate in seeing some of my creative goals through to completion with a fairly good level of self-trust. I'd like to develop even greater confidence, set some big goals that scare me, and know with 100% confidence that I have access to all it takes to achieve them.*

f) *I've made creative dreams into realities many times. I love the feeling of creating with the end in mind and of living in alignment with my sense of calling. Even though my confidence is strong, I know I can turn bigger, more expansive visions into realities, with gifts for others, not just me. I know that venturing beyond my comfort zone can become as routine as writing in my journal, and I look forward to taking more constructive, creative risks in the service of my dreams.*

7. **Describe your current creative dreams and specific goals.**

a) *I have a sense that I'm being pulled to create somehow, but I have no clear, personal, creative goals. In fact, I'm so busy that sometimes I resent feeling I should have more goals in my life.*

b) *I have a vague notion of something I'd like to achieve creatively, but little sense of how to take my goal-setting further. Most of the time, a feeling of being overwhelmed prevents me from getting started on anything creative. At least I acknowledge where I'm at. I can see that yearning to be creative, yet feeling vague and blocked, is a legitimate place to start from.*

c) *I know very generally what I'd like to accomplish, but don't have the details in place. My dream feels too big for me right now. I wish I could move past this tension of dreaming on a grand scale and fearing it. I'm ready to become more specific and less fearful.*

d) *I have at least one somewhat specific creative goal, and I think I stand a chance of achieving it. I don't have a clear plan, however. Setting goals has never been a problem, but following through is the area where in the past I've repeatedly fallen down.*

e) *I have goals and a general plan. I need to make the details more specific and am ready to begin.*

f) *I have clear, specific goals and a specific plan. I'm ready to take the action steps required to make my goals realities.*

8. **Describe your plans for achieving your creative goals.**

a) *No goals, no plans. At least I acknowledge this!*

b) *Very little thought given to goal-setting and planning so far. I feel resistance in this area.*

c) *A vague plan for achieving vague goals.*

d) *Some planning in place.*

e) *Ballpark planning in place, on a timeline, but more specifics needed.*

f) *A vision clearly in place, with a "work backwards" plan: a series of due dates on a detailed calendar.*

9. **To what extent do you know the support people and resources you require for your creative progress?**

a) I need support and resources? (Ha, ha.) Okay, I guess I've never taken my creativity seriously enough to think on this level.

b) Very little. I know I need to hone my craft skills, but I'm not sure how to do that. I feel highly self-conscious about seeking help. I'm not even sure if I should bother.

c) I'd like to get better at what I do creatively, but my experiences in the past were negative and I'm reluctant to reach out for help again, especially given my current age and/or situation.

d) I have a basic sense of what I need to work on, just not how I'm going to get support for it. It's the same with my constructive thinking skills: I know I'd like to change my thought patterns. Reading this book is a start.

e) I have a reasonably good sense of the support I need for my skill development overall, including "attitude skills" — i.e., building resiliency. I'm eager to put some plans in place to grow.

f) I have a strong, clear sense of the resources I require for creative growth. These include resources in all relevant areas of skill: in positive, vision-based thinking, in my craft, in business, etc. I'm already receiving support and have a strong desire and clear plan to access more of it. I understand that receiving help expands my creative possibilities. It's a mark of strength, not weakness.

10. **How "on track" do you feel creatively? To what extent are you taking action to follow through on your plans?**

a) Not at all.

b) Somewhat (at best).

c) I occasionally get a clear sense through my yearning and my desire, and when I see I've done something well. But there's no consistency.

d) I feel I'm developing a sense of being on track, of living "on purpose" creatively. It's taken me time, and I'm moving forward. I'm beginning to take action.

e) Increasingly I feel on track, even while I don't know how I'm going to make my creative goals realities. I've been taking steady, small steps in the direction of my creative dreams. One day at a time.

f) I'm on track, making full use of my resources. I take action on a daily basis, following through on my scheduled creative tasks.

After you've finished circling the answers that most closely correspond with what's true for you, take a few minutes to notice patterns and to make connections relevant to your core beliefs and creative desires—to your goals, plans, resources, and overall trust in yourself to follow through. Which answers are farthest along the continuum (D through F)? Which are closest to the beginning (A through C)? Take note, without being self-critical, of where you are in your journey of learning to trust yourself creatively. Is your trust level high or low? Is it somewhere in between? Up until now, have you trusted yourself to set goals and to follow through and fulfill them? If you don't have clear and specific goals and plans right now, that's good information to have. The exercises in this book will help you to set some.

The more we trust ourselves creatively, the more confident we become. Confidence leads to more purposeful and effective action. After you've reflected on your quiz answers, take stock of how creatively confident you feel.

What is your overall level of creative confidence at this moment?

a) *I have none.*

b) *I have very little.*

c) *My creative confidence is inconsistent and ultimately unsatisfying be-*

cause it only applies when I'm in my comfort zone.

d) *I have a moderate level of confidence. I've been trying to feel more confident, but it's hard because sometimes I feel so far from achieving my creative goals.*

e) *I have a good level of confidence, and I continue looking for ways to keep it growing.*

f) *I feel strongly confident in my creative work. However, I could always use a greater sense of assuredness and determination in the face of obstacles, including criticism and rejection.*

I invite you to take a reading of your creative confidence from time to time as you complete the exercises in this book and continue building skills and wins in your life beyond these pages. If and when your confidence wanes, return to the quiz questions above and look for those which seem to nudge you to move along a continuum. Building confidence requires patience and the repetition of constructive behaviors and thinking. Don't berate yourself for lacking confidence—simply put the habits in place to build it.

The Fruit of Persistence

The flicker, remember, is a member of the woodpecker family, and woodpeckers hold a large place in the world of avian folklore. The Norse ancestors saw the red streak on a woodpecker's head as a link to their god Thor's fiery red hair and his thunderbolts. They likened its beak to Thor's hammer, and drew a parallel between the holes it makes in the trees and those caused by lightning. The woodpecker is a symbol of great power; its habitforce is divine. In his book *Flights of Fancy: Birds in Myth, Legend and Superstition*, author Peter Tate points to an association made in Scandinavian mythology between the woodpecker (in old German, *Bienwulf*, meaning "bee eater") and Beowulf, the hero who slew the monster Grendel. My favorite of Tate's collected folk beliefs on the woodpecker comes from Germany, where traditionally people believed it to possess secret knowledge of where to find the magic herb springwort. If "the entrance to a woodpecker's nest was blocked up, the bird would straightaway fly off to find the herb and hold it against the obstruction, whereupon a hole would immediately appear. Springwort was therefore ideally suited to open locks."

And blocks.

Most people who feel creatively blocked and frustrated are unhappy because on some level they've stopped believing in their own potential. As a young woman I felt most torn and sad when I was filled with creative energy and yet lacking in a living structure that could channel it. I had not yet learned that the only way I could fail as a writer was not to write. Eventually I discovered how a daily journal practice created pathways of discipline and trust in my mind. It also helped me to reconnect with a sense of fun, play, authenticity, and laughter. To regain creative confidence, I had to learn how to become like a child.

Trailing Clouds of Glory

Small children trust themselves to play. No one has to teach a preschool child to create—the creative life force lives naturally, lightly, and freely in tiny humans through the marks they make in the world: snow angels, footprints in mud, crayon lines on living room walls, and spaghetti handprints. Little children are naturally brilliant; they know how to make themselves happy—that state of being which Aristotle saw as a central purpose in human life. Listen to a group of youngsters for a time and you'll hear humming, singing, and whispering—their laughter is part of the rhythm of the world. I've heard it said that a young child laughs one hundred times per day; contrast that with the fewer than twenty times per day of an average adult. The world of early childhood is full of quests, of mark making and delight. And for a while those marks are honored; think of the countless art masterpieces you've seen proudly displayed with fridge magnets. Children themselves are magnets for the creative life force.

Unfortunately "mark" is a word redefined for children when they enter school, and it suddenly applies to the act of being measured and assessed. When children come to associate marks with judgment, and to allow marks to dictate emotion and a sense of self-worth, the laughter fades. Even high marks have their trip wires.

Learning to attach happiness to high achievement is one of the mixed blessings of traditional schooling. Celebrating success is one of life's sweet spots, and we've all felt the rush of delight when our work has earned favorable results. But it's dangerous to become reliant upon external praise to build confidence. Real confidence comes from a deeper place within—from faith and meaning. By and large, schools are happy and industrious places. It would be an understatement to say that good teachers bring considerable learning, expertise, and gifts to the classroom. And great teachers are artists at their work. They offer encouragement to their students, endeavoring to help build their students' confidence and to elicit genuine curiosity and strong, abiding, and enthusiastic efforts. It's quite a challenge. I know, because I taught among the best for twenty years. In my classroom I worked hard to award marks fairly, connecting them meaningfully to evidence of learning. Yet I never became entirely comfortable with the marking process.

Like many teachers, I wanted to provide feedback without numbers—but we live in a numbers world. We haven't yet learned to create an education system that doesn't ultimately speak in percentages and grades. For me, marking nagged like an unhealed injury. "I'm not marking *you*," I'd say, "just the piece of paper." Then I'd sigh, knowing that, regardless of my sincerity—for I always saw the shining potential in my students, I always saw that the spirit in them was bigger and more powerful than any circumstance or product of their effort—my students didn't see the marking process with the same eyes. Too often, they allowed their marks to determine their emotional responses. High marks made them "high," often taking them outside of what was meaningful in their work; when their marks weren't perceived to be high enough, anxiety set in, separating them from the potential for making beneficial meaning. Who could blame them? Their response was learned, not innate. Sometimes the adults in their lives also had difficulty appreciating that academic marks are simply data: neither inherently bad nor good. It's what we *do* with our data that counts. We are empowered or disempowered by our stories. Either way, we create them.

Years ago, it took a physical disease and an unconsciously engineered pattern of heartbreak for me to see what I'd created, and to open fully to meeting myself on the pages of my life. While I don't wish my own catalytic experiences on anyone else, I've come to own and reframe them as the best things that could have happened to me, given the track I was on. I'm grateful for the spiritual wake-up calls, and for my own self-discipline in showing up at the page each day. Journaling and reflecting honestly, visioning wholeheartedly, being prepared, finally, to act on visions—these are among life's healing gifts, and they're certainly not exclusive to artists. As Leonard Cohen sings, "There is a crack in everything. That's how the light gets in." When we learn to see our wounds as sacred, we experience the lightness to transcend them and create—to be empowered and unbound by circumstance.

Red Feather

A flicker sounds above me in a broken tree, an extraordinary bird well disguised among the ordinary. Flickers live in my urban neighborhood, but only when I found one dead several years ago did I discover their subtle, breathtaking beauty. The little bird's motionless presence in my yard compelled me: the fawn-and-white speckled breast; the yellow hidden inside the striped wings; the sleek black tail feathers; the red-streaked head with its black crescent moon at the throat. I returned many times to study it, not wanting to remove it from the place where it had fallen.

A gift.

Each aspect of the flicker's appearance bears symbolic meaning in at least one culture. For example, the red feathers on its head have a particular import for the Pueblo people, who hold that a red feather on a prayer stick means the same energy used for war can be used for healing.

Self-knowledge is found on a healing path. It keeps us seeking and finding, visioning and creating anew. Gifts are gifts because we make them so. Choosing not to be at war with oneself, with life, but to consciously and courageously create and heal, in any circumstance, is a true gift. In accepting it, we begin to make a paradigm shift and learn to accept forward movement, beyond the established comfort zone, into new territory.

At midlife, I made an active decision to release an old way of being and to make marks in a new way. The word "mark" comes to us through the Saxons: *merke*, meaning "sign" or "boundary." The Norse word *morke* also meant "forest"—often the marker of a frontier. Latin *margo* meant "margin," and Old Irish *mruig* meant "borderland." I've chosen to live and create at the borderland between the known and the unknown. Making friends with fear, I've come to accept its presence as one which tells me when I'm at that place. And something in me strives ever to expand the territory, to live at the frontier and push beyond old boundaries.

As a fiction writer, I ask my characters to take me to the emotional frontiers of knowing, seeing, and experiencing. As an artist and a coach in creativity, dream building, and transformation, I now take risks to serve others in ways leading positively and continually to growth: ways my young-woman self yearned for and my child self believed in completely. In the melting snow, I feel that child emerge in me again, my life a spring, regardless of "conditions."

Where is your frontier? Invite your fear to show you.

Your creative dream isn't big enough unless it scares you. What dream scares you enough, and holds enough gifts for you and others, that you know it's worthy—not only of your time and efforts, but of *you*? What one action could you take today, resolutely, for your dream?

**Claiming The Flicker's Gifts:
Trust and Confidence**

Exercise 1: Commit to a Daily Journal Practice

By now it's obvious that starting a journal practice, or recommitting to one, is a key exercise for this chapter. Here are the essentials: Aim to write a few pages a day and simply see what you have to say. Write at the same time each day—I strongly recommend the early morning (get up earlier if you have to). Be honest. Let the words flow freely and don't judge them. If you're a writer, remember that journaling is *not* composition. In Chapter 4, I'll outline additional journal techniques that you can add to your practice. For now, simply commit to maintaining a constructive, private, and reflective daily writing habit for ninety days.

One more thing: I *strongly* recommend that at the end of each free-flowing journal session, you list ten things that you are grateful for. This way, regardless of the writing content and your associated feelings, you build the habit of reconnecting with gratitude, abundance, and a very positive attitude as you move into your day. Creating experiences from a place of gratitude is vital to joyful, fulfilling living.

Exercise 2: Reprogram Your Inner Playlist

You can change the thought patterns in your subconscious mind, by literally replacing old, learned beliefs with new ones. Research shows that it takes about ninety days. I invite you to get rid of unwanted thoughts—to choose the new paradigm from which you desire to create. This process requires open-mindedness, effort, commitment, and repetition.

Return to your Chapter 1 exercises and find the lists you made of empowering and disempowering beliefs about your own creativity. From the "empowering" column, choose any ideas you'd like to reinforce and write them out as present-tense affirmations. For example, "I am so happy and grateful now that I've grown to trust, enjoy, and develop my beautiful gift of singing through choir and private lessons. I love singing!" Select only beliefs that make you feel great just thinking about them. (If you don't have any yet, don't write any yet.) Next, have a good look again at your disempowering beliefs. You need to know exactly what you're dealing with. Up until now, those beliefs have functioned like magnets in attracting your present reality. If you wish to change that reality, it's time to replace the old "program." Turn each negative statement into a positive affirmation by conveying its polar opposite. For example, if one of your beliefs is "I suck at drawing," then change it to "I am so happy and grateful that my drawing skills are strong and growing." Imagine what your strong drawing skills would look like. Picture your own beautiful sketches on the pages of your mind as you repeat your affirmation. Feel how you would feel in seeing them manifest. Create a *future memory* of a fulfilling creative experience.

Even as your self-doubt inwardly screams and threatens to undermine your completion of the activity, persist until you've transformed each negative belief into a positive affirmation and mental picture. If possible, bring uplifting emotion to your imagining. Begin each positive statement by expressing joy and gratitude. Your specific language choices are important; I work with my clients for quite a while until we've got the wording just right. Take time to find words that feel beneficially charged and reassuring. Your affirmation list is a powerful game changer when you commit to working with it routinely.

Once you've written your list, recite it ten times in a calm and soothing voice into your phone or other recording device. Commit to listening to your affirmations at least twice a day—morning and night. Play them at times when you can focus on them. Listening to your affirmations puts you on an alpha brain-wave frequency, which helps the information to become ingrained.

Exercise 3: Set a Creative Goal

What would you *love* to accomplish creatively? What would you create if you knew you couldn't fail? Take a risk and write it down. Say yes to it. The very act of deciding to *have* a creative goal—a dream!—attacks the old paradigm of self-doubt. Boldly decide what you would love and prepare to take action for it, regardless of your fears. Facing fears greatly diminishes them. I have heard many times, from those I trust, that if your dream doesn't scare you it isn't big enough!

Review your creative goal (or goals) each day, and imagine how you would feel if that goal were already accomplished. Don't think about how you'll achieve it, simply focus on what it feels like *already fulfilled*. We will go into more detail on specific visioning practices in Chapter 4.

Key Ideas

Review the statements below. Choose three to five of the most helpful ideas and add them to your personal favorites collection, where you'll see them every day.

- Constructive habits build self-trust. Trust builds faith, and trust and faith build confidence. Confidence is essential to the fulfillment of creative dreams.
- Daily journal practice builds self-trust and opens the channel to discovery.
- A relaxed mind is a creative mind. Take time for quiet reflection each day.
- Single-pointed focus marshals energy; it directs and increases personal power in the service of creative dreams.

- Journal writing leads to greater creative flow, synchronicity, and intuition.
- In a journal, allowing yourself to be vulnerable ultimately fosters courage, compassion, and connection—vital attributes of any thriving person.
- When you become like a child, you remember that joy, play, and authenticity are in your nature. So is creative confidence.
- Discipline is the ability to give yourself a command and follow it. Confidence comes from trusting yourself to follow through on your own plans.
- Putting a routine creative practice first in the day ensures follow-through.
- Self-reliance sets the stage for the persistence required to achieve creative goals.
- Confidence comes from within, not without; self-reliance trumps praise.
- Your thoughts and words shape your reality. You have the power to choose them.
- The same energy used for waging war can be used for healing. Only you can decide how to use your energy.
- Experience is simply data. It's what we do with our data that counts.
- Make friends with fear.
- Decide what you want and take action for it.

Chapter 3
The Robin: Freeing Your Authenticity

To be yourself in a world that is constantly trying to make you something else is the greatest accomplishment.
—Ralph Waldo Emerson

Your time is limited, so don't waste it living someone else's life....
Don't let the noise of others' opinions drown out your own inner voice. And most important, have the courage to follow your heart and intuition. They somehow already know what you truly want to become.
Everything else is secondary.
—Steve Jobs

Clues to Character

We can all learn from the qualities of the robin, a feisty little bird. As creative beings, we can take direction from its significance as a harbinger of spring and new growth. Each of us has spring inside us, including memories of that most obvious spring: childhood. Why go back there? After all, it is often a time of awkwardness, confusion, and turmoil. For me, the answer is clear: We go back through childhood memories to rediscover the signposts of our character, and in this way we gain strength. Through memory, we find clues to our early sense of authenticity and purpose.

What exactly does "authenticity" mean in the context of living an adult life? To my mind, living authentically as a grown-up means feeling, thinking, and acting in alignment with one's core values and a sense of mission. It's endeavoring to live one's best and truest version of oneself, and creating the conditions to make that happen.

Being authentic does not mean we always meet our mark, but that, regardless of our current circumstances, we love our aim. Indeed, we must learn to *live* our aim. Going off course is human nature; being aware of when we're on the wrong track, and of what we can do to get back on the right one, is the divine in action within us. Positive, passionate, and purposeful use of the imagination can be a superpower: it holds the key to keeping us on track to creative fulfillment.

In adulthood, sometimes we have experiences that cause us to doubt our own legitimacy on the creative path. Childhood memories can help us to counter self-doubt, as we reflect on significant moments in our lives which have, even subtly, pointed to a calling. The robin is an emblem not only of spring but of individual expression: each robin sings its own distinct song. Childhood memories remind us of our music.

In the section that follows, I offer you several fleeting episodes from my own childhood journey as encouragement to follow the pebbles back to the early signposts of *your* unique character. By revisiting your memories, particularly those charged with emotion—especially joy—you honor your distinct and beautiful calling; you recognize it anew, with a view to purposefully heeding it. The clearer your sense of authentic mission, the better able you'll be to withstand the challenges that you encounter along the creative path.

A Bookish Bird

My mother claims that shortly before I was born she received a message that she'd have a girl and call her Robin. Just like that. One of those "mental downloads" people get. Although in those days the computer term didn't exist—when I was born, Dr. Martin Luther King, Jr., was still voicing the shining poetry of justice and Neil Armstrong hadn't yet walked on the moon.

I'd like to tell you I was reading for several years before kindergarten, but I wasn't. Neither was I a left-handed savant, or a child possessed of uncanny abilities. I didn't see angels in a tree. My early childhood education included routine exposure to television reruns of *The Dick Van Dyke Show, Flipper,* and *I Love Lucy,* as well as new episodes of *That Girl, I Dream of Jeannie,* and *The Beverly Hillbillies.* (This last, when simultaneously broadcast through our kitchen radio, confused me, as I believed the tiny Clampetts lived inside our TV.) Each night I sat on the pea-green couch between my twenty-something parents, academics whose family life had begun a little sooner than they'd anticipated. They cuddled with me after dinner as we laughed at our favorite characters' antics in that golden interval before my bedtime and their evening studies.

In the sixties, my neural pathways were paved with the stuff of American sitcoms and, of course, cartoons. Unlike many first-world children today, whose early "programming" may include Kumon Math, Suzuki violin lessons, elite athletic training, or immersion in at least one additional language, my early childhood education included an almost perfect mastery of *The Flintstones.* I know I'm not alone.

Even more than television, I loved books—everything about them—and I begged my mother to read to me each night. She had her own books to ponder in that strange, silent way of adults—creased tomes with mysterious titles like *Renaissance England, English Romantic Poetry,* and *Jude the Obscure.* But naturally, I believed my books were better. Some had large, indestructibly hard pages which were wonderful to point to, and my "what happens next" predictions about the stories were almost always right. Not only did they feature great pictures and stories, with wicked queens and trolls and billy goats, anguished princes, talking frogs, fairy princesses, and a young David with his slingshot (beside a weirdly thrilling headless Goliath), but my books were capable of *much* more than merely being read.

At a moment's notice my books could splay themselves obediently into the structural walls of a castle built of alphabet blocks and plastic stacking cups, an upended xylophone, hammering-pegs, and more bright blocks, bounded by a moat of Ladybird-brand underpants and itchy leotards better suited to topography than legwear. My books were capable of withstanding being flung right into the box beside my Gina doll from Italy, my bride doll, and Jasper, the grinning bear from Alberta with a constantly bobbing head. My books also tasted interesting: the thin layer of plastic vaguely detectible over the cardboard, smooth and cold to my tongue—a little like the lobby window, but not as grime-bitter.

My grandparents owned a bookstore in the late sixties, and they often brought me treasures. One poetry book disturbed me, though it was nice to hear my Yorkshire grandfather read "Who Killed Cock Robin?"

Gulp.

"'I,' said the Sparrow, 'with my bow and arrow.'"

I loved the sound of Grandpa Blackburn's gravelly old English voice, even when his words alarmed me. Something in me flinched, knowing it was wrong to kill a robin. Of course, at that point, I wasn't familiar with the many traditional beliefs surrounding this chirpy little bird. In *Flights of Fancy*, Peter Tate writes, "Such is the fondness felt for robins that there are many taboos against killing or harming one." He recounts the Norse conviction that the bird was beloved by Thor, so that if the bird or its nest was deliberately destroyed, the perpetrator would be "annihilated" by lightning or fire. Tate reveals that in one Christian tradition, a "widespread story tells how the robin shared Jesus' agony on the cross, and, as a result, carries a drop of God's blood in its veins to this day." As a consequence, in some places, it was considered not just a source of bad luck but a sin to harm a robin.

At age four, however, I didn't know or care a fig about those ideas. As I gazed solemnly upon the arrow stuck brightly into Cock Robin's red heart, the only thing that bothered me was that the slain bird had *my name*. Why did we have to share that name? *Why?!* For the first time, a book caused me to question my identity. To make matters worse, when I entered school, adults and children alike often remarked that I had a boy's name. And my full name was a source of amusement to my classmates; they would skip behind me, calling "Robin Blackbird" and parodying my gestures. How I wished that I really *could* be an edgy blackbird. Then again, blackbirds got baked in a pie. Thanks to a Jackson Five cover, I claimed "Rockin' Robin" as the one positive cultural reference associated with my name, bouncing inwardly to every "tweet, tweedle-lee-dee." Quickly I found a place in class as a comic performer—then, later, as a not-so-funny one. That plump-bellied little loudmouth bird got me into trouble sometimes. The more I rocked in the treetops, the more prone I was to being teased. When teased, my way of coping was to lean into books all the more, and into writing—my happy place—where I experienced the most satisfaction in growing.

I was socially nervous, although few would have guessed it from my behavior. When stuck for words in a playground conversation, I once called "Shut up!" because it was all I could think of. On the first morning of kindergarten I grabbed another child's block—not out of greed or covetousness, but because (I still remember) it just looked fun to play with. Thus, my earliest memory involving a teacher is of being busted. I had to stand with my hands on my head in the middle of the room while the young, first-year shepherdess arranged the others in a circle. Later, I would fall in love with my kindergarten teacher in a prescient display of Stockholm Syndrome. When she arrived at school one day with newly coiffed and fashionable hair, I cut my hair off too, in solidarity—with nail scissors. I wanted to be like Miss S. in every way. That included being a "real" reader. What's more, I wanted to be a writer.

My dad took me on my first-ever visit to the public library, and the experience marked me for life. I still remember the flutter of wings in my tummy: the magic feeling of standing among so many books. I knew I'd write some myself. My first book came through me that very afternoon while my baby brother napped. My mother scribed my debut work of fiction, *A Bird in the Library*. Eagerly, I illustrated the slim volume in compensatingly thick Crayola crayons: my first foray into self-publishing.

During my years at elementary school, I wrote and delivered impassioned speeches on the arts and the power of the imagination—or "make-believe," as I called it—delighting in fancy and a sense of limitlessness. I won contests, which put me on shaky ground socially. My speeches did not make me popular, but they gave me a palpable feeling of progress. There was a spiritual component to my efforts which I sensed at the time but couldn't fully understand or articulate.

I also wrote copious stories, which an exceptionally dedicated teacher typed for me in a thick-at-last volume, compassionately honoring my quest to be taken seriously. He must have seen that, while I did have a few good friends, I was socially awkward; while I could readily appear confident, making people laugh at my stage antics, I didn't yet have a sense of humor about myself. He also saw my burning desire to write. Thanks to that teacher's supportive efforts, when I stood up in class to read my work, I experienced elation in beholding my classmates' very positive responses. I savored the feeling of being able to do something that I loved and do it well—something which connected me with people. Making meaningful connections was going to become increasingly important in my life.

In grade school, I could be just as callous in my behavior toward other children as they were to me. Like everyone, I thought I was special. We were all, at times, sparrows, shooting arrows around the schoolyard. We were also robins, each one of us in possession of a unique call. Often, we didn't recognize our gifts. Now I see my early love of writing as a harbinger of my own renewal through story and a lifelong dedication to the arts. It was, like my other experiences in the arts, a spiritual marker. I see my early social awkwardness as preparation for helping others; I had to learn about the inner world of the human spirit by experiencing the pain and resilience of perceiving myself as an outsider—to break through the illusion of feeling separate. My bookishness was a sign of my calling, but so was my social vulnerability.

At midlife, I withdrew from teaching to write full-time, but eventually I sought more of a balance between art and service. This time, balance would find a new form: I came to know that I was meant to not only continue as a writer but also serve other creatively inspired people through direct connection. Following my heart caused me to grow, yet again affirming for me that when we trust and follow our dreams, navigating even the deepest of fears to do so, our dreams take us to the next stage in our authentic becoming.

More Thoughts on Character and Calling

Like many, I am still awed by Apple founder Steve Jobs' 2005 commencement speech at Stanford University. I'm grateful that I live in a time when, at the click of a button, I can listen to this visionary game changer talk about his path: despite everything, he always trusted his own curiosity, and that is the most vital message of his legacy. I love listening to Jobs speak about the impossibility of "connecting the dots" in our lives by looking forward. It's only in memory that we see the signposts of our calling, our own authentic character and unique mission. "You have to trust in something," says Jobs—"your gut, destiny, life, karma, whatever. This approach has never let me down, and it has made all the difference in my life." Certainly, the approach allowed him to reframe the potentially disempowering experience of being fired from his own company at age thirty, to one of shifting from the "heaviness of being successful" to "the lightness of being a beginner again." Moreover, being a beginner freed Jobs "to enter one of the most creative periods" of his life.

In Buddhist dharma, emphasis is placed on cultivating a beginner's mind. Each day, as we awaken to the sound of birdsong, we have an opportunity to begin again—to fall in love with life once more. One of the paradoxical gifts of mastery in a chosen area of passion is realizing that living in alignment with one's calling, and leading with one's strengths, can help sustain a sense of freshness and joy in being *ever* a beginner. Jobs sums it up quite simply: "You've got to find what you love."

Finding what we love is about finding who we truly are. In preparing to write this chapter, I revisited a book I discovered many years ago, one that has been essential to my ongoing process of connecting the dots: James Hillman's *The Soul's Code: In Search of Character and Calling*. The author, an eminent Jungian psychologist, makes a case for paying attention to childhood's significant moments—those times when, "out of nowhere, a fascination, a peculiar turn of events struck like an annunciation: This is what I must do, this is what I've got to have. This is who I am." He goes on to state that for many, "the call may have been more like gentle pushings in the stream" in which they "drifted unknowingly to a particular spot on the bank." A central message of his book is that we find the clues to our own unique mission in "humdrum miracles when the mark of character appears." In remembering those shining moments, suddenly, more clues to our purpose may be revealed. In today's culture, Hillman says, it's easy to become distracted by memories of childhood traumas and miss the subtler, vitally important clues to personal calling and purpose.

Hillman introduces childhood case studies of a broad range of people famous for their contributions. He also includes this brief discussion of Plato's Myth of Er, one of the final stories in *The Republic*:

> Each person enters the world called.... The soul of each of us is given a unique daimon before we are born, and it has selected an image or pattern that we live on earth. This soul-companion, the daimon, guides us here; in the process of arrival, however, we forget all that took place and believe we come empty into this world.... Then, the myth implies, we must attend very carefully to childhood to catch early glimpses of the daimon in

> action, to grasp its intentions and not block its way....
> A calling may be postponed, avoided, intermittently missed. It may also possess you completely. Whatever; eventually it will out. It makes its claim. The daimon does not go away.

Keep this myth in mind as you connect the dots of your early experience, substituting for "daimon" whatever it is that you feel accounts for your own will force, passion, and authentic sense of mission (whether established or emerging).

Hillman's case studies are fascinating; not all of the "acorns" that develop into mighty "oak trees" are obvious. While some of the figures he describes, such as virtuoso violinist Yehudi Menuhin, displayed an early passion for the means to fulfill their callings, others began life looking and behaving very differently from their future selves. The discrepancies between child and adult inclinations and behaviors themselves tell a story. For example, the writer Colette would do anything *but* write when she was growing up; yet, despite her adamant desire *not* to write, she kept the tools of her future craft around her—and one day would describe those writing tools at great length and in sensuous detail. The legendary Spanish bullfighter Manolete began life as a timid, frightened child, as did the future leader of India Mohandas Gandhi. Hillman suggests that an intuitive sense of the scale to which their missions would take them contributed to these two boys' early inhibitions.

Evidence of a particular inhibition causing a child to retreat can be just as significant a marker of an authentic calling as is the "unexpected annunciation" that reveals a passion. Hillman also includes examples of a childhood "obsessional desire for the tools that make realization possible." I love his account of Menuhin at age four matter-of-factly telling his parents that he wanted to study violin with a renowned musician, and that he wanted a fine instrument to get started on. When little Yehudi later received a toy violin for his birthday, the child flew into a rage. In his mind, he was not little!

And, according to Hillman, neither was his daimon—nor is anyone else's, for that matter.

Hillman cites creativity specialist and Harvard professor of psychiatry Albert Rothenberg as having isolated one common denominator in the personalities of exceptional creative achievers: motivation. "He rules out intelligence, temperament, personality type, introversion, inheritance, early environment, inspiration, obsession, mental disorder: '…only motivation is…present in all.'" I find that news reassuring. Motivation is a signpost we can look for in our childhood and young adult memories; it's also something we can learn to access, cultivate, and build on in maturity. One of the reasons I love coaching is that it's a dynamic, life-affirming, and expansive process of helping people harness the power of their own motivation. Living in alignment with a sense of authenticity and creative purpose is a powerful catalyst for each one of us, as we grow in making meaningful contributions to the world around us.

An Invitation to Connect the Dots

Working in education for many years has reinforced in me the belief that every child is gifted. We all arrive with special qualities. You were, and are, a one-of-a-kind contributor. Learning to recognize your gifts and to take action in alignment with your calling is a lifelong process—and one with great benefits not only to you but to others.

I encourage you to read through the prompts below and highlight the ones you feel have particular relevance to your creative journey. Respond to these highlighted prompts in your journal. As you begin the experience of making useful connections, linking the dots of character and calling, I invite you to pause and consider what exactly you desire for yourself creatively at this point in your life. What information do you seek in your journey back in time? What revelations from your past can help you in forming your present goals?

1. What strong memories, if any, do you have of early childhood? In those memories, can you find evidence of alignment between your behavior as a child and your present creative interests and passions?

2. One of the things I realized in looking back at my early childhood was that, before external pressures came to bear, I was naturally a risk taker. This was quite a revelation to me, as in adulthood I'd often blamed myself for playing too safe. Are there any moments in your past where you witnessed yourself taking creative risks, for better or (seemingly) for worse? List any you can remember that caused you to feel a strong level of either success or discomfort. Both outcomes can be richly instructive.

3. Did you have a moment of "annunciation" when you just knew what you wanted to do creatively with your life?

4. Did you yearn for particular tools? If so, what were they? Do your memories of those desired items or conditions connect in any way to the tools you desire now?

5. In her research into the neuroscience of creativity at the University of Iowa, Nancy Andreasen, M.D. and Ph.D., notes that a common experience of highly creative individuals is their willingness to work harder than most other people—likely because they enjoy their chosen work. Can you remember any times in childhood when you went the extra mile in the service of something you loved? What about more recent times?

6. The areas that frightened us in childhood can be our teachers now, pointing us back to the very things we need to do and face, and to the places we can still go, in order to grow and heed our call. Sometimes fears show up markedly in early life, such as Gandhi's experience, as reported by Hillman, of being "a short, thin, ailing, ugly, and frightened child, afraid especially of snakes, ghosts, and the dark." Mythologist Joseph Campbell reminds us, "The very cave you are afraid

to enter turns out to be the source of what you are looking for." Which of your childhood fears seemed innate? Which ones developed as a result of your experience of being either unsuccessful or successful? Did you overcome your fears? Do you still have old fears you feel compelled to overcome? What cave holds your treasure?

7. From two wise teachers, Mary Morrissey and Peggy McColl, I've learned about the work of psychologist, writer, and transformational coach Gay Hendricks. In his book *The Big Leap: Conquer Your Hidden Fear and Take Life to the Next Level*, Hendricks has identified four reasons why people don't succeed: (a) feeling fundamentally flawed; (b) fear of abandonment and disloyalty; (c) fear of the burden of success; and (d) fear of outshining (i.e., surpassing the achievement level of one or more people you love). Did any of those fears crop up for you as you followed your curiosities and passions in childhood? What about now, in adulthood?

8. Looking back, what strengths did you display growing up? If this is a difficult question for you to answer, I encourage you to put yourself in the shoes of a loving and compassionate visitor from the future, and imagine a scene in which your young self appears to you. What strikes you as memorable about the child you see before you? What qualities tug at your heartstrings? What impresses you? What, if anything, causes you to feel concern for this child? What aspects of this child need protecting and strengthening? What strengths are hidden? Why? Talk with this child, and listen carefully. Are there any toxic thoughts that need releasing in either the child or adult versions of you? I gently urge you to let go of any old negativity now by choosing to feel and believe opposite thoughts. Recognize your power in being a guardian to this child. You can right any wrongs of the past by releasing the effects which no longer serve you. Embrace and encourage

the child who has found the courage to appear before you in your mind; take that dear child with you consciously, now, as you move forward, claiming all of your life as immeasurably meaningful and valuable. Give yourself permission to have faith in the precious child within you, and in the adult you continue to become each day.

Living Authentically Now

In the first few sections of this chapter on the robin, harbinger of spring, we have looked at the springtime of our childhoods. The less obvious, but more powerful, spring inside each of us is that part which seeks growth regardless of the candle tally on our birthday cake. The remainder of this chapter focuses on heeding the call to live our own particular mission here and now. We all have spring inside us. That part of us which seeks expansion, our pure creativity, is ageless. If you doubt that, think of all the artists who have stayed fully energized and prolific in their work, well into their senior years: Georgia O'Keeffe, Ansel Adams, Lawren Harris, Henri Matisse, Martha Graham, Pablo Picasso, P.D. James, and Alice Munro, to name several. Think of Frank McCourt, who had memoirs in him throughout thirty years of teaching school and only afterward, at last, made those books manifest. Think of Alan Bradley, the best-selling Canadian murder mystery writer, who created the precocious and charming sleuth Flavia de Luce after his "retirement."

We can all choose growth at any age, as the robin colorfully reminds us—and there has never been a better time than now. The robin is known for the bright red hue on its breast and belly, a color that, according to *Animal Speak* author Ted Andrews, is connected to kundalini energy, which the yogis believe resides within us at the root chakra, the life force. In energy medicine, another chakra, located at the throat, is considered our place of creative will; it corresponds to a light blue color. Andrews writes, "The robin lays a distinctive powder-blue egg. This color is often used to activate the throat center in humans." Such activation opens the channel for our own will force and creativity. The throat chakra is the communication center of the body. When energy stops flowing freely here, creative individuals suffer, their music bottled deep inside them. If you yearn to express yourself creatively and feel blocked, I recommend you supplement your practice of the exercises in this book by receiving energy healing with a qualified practitioner. Reiki and other etheric practices may be of benefit to you; creative movement, yoga, and vocalization can help, too.

The power of one's will and imagination determine much for the artist, the innovator, the breakthrough-maker. Traditionally it was thought of as bad luck to steal a robin's egg. If you worry that, in the course of your life, your own creative power has been "stolen" from you as the result of emotional injury, think again. It *is* still there inside you, and you *can* reclaim it. Put some red and robin's-egg blue into your creative space to remind you of your gifts—among them your life force, your will, and the creative power of your imagination. Experiment with wearing the robin's colors to remind you of your unique potential. Establish your intent to be who you truly are, and then, in your imagination—and in your whole life—become that person.

Harness the Power of Your Imagination

Here is a crucial point in your study and application of the material in this book: your power to concentrate your will in service of your mighty imagination is the key to actualizing your vision over time. You must learn to concentrate your mind in holding, emotionalizing, and "five-sensorizing" a vision of yourself already living the creative life you desire. The feeling that you bring to this work is of great importance; your state of mind and emotion must be positively aligned with how you believe you would feel in living your desired creative life. You can learn to make your will strong. You can also learn to be calm as you employ your will to sustain an "imaginal" experience—that is, an extended, strong experience of being inside an imagined vision.

One of the metaphysical writers I return to time and again is the deeply instructive Neville Goddard. In *The Power of Awareness*, he explains that a change in consciousness must occur before any of us can change in the outer world: "To be transformed, the whole basis of your thoughts must change. But your thoughts cannot change unless you have *new ideas*, for you think from your ideas. All transformation begins with an intense, burning desire to be transformed." In adulthood, those of us with a burning desire to create can take heart. Transformation—which requires both an act of claiming (indeed, *re*claiming) and one of releasing—is possible.

When you revisit memories of your childhood and youth for clues to your early creative strengths, curiosities, passions, and calling, remember this key point: while a sense of calling can appear quite vividly at the beginning of a human life, rarely is a child or young adult able to fully heed it. Children are naturally imaginative and certainly they're creative—even brilliant—but it takes maturity to learn how to harness the power of the human imagination constructively. In order to clarify and realize our visions, generally we need age and experience on our side. I trust that I am not alone in recognizing this as good news. I love these words of inspiration, by the prolific American artist and polymath Walter Russell, on the related subjects of genius and maturity:

> I believe sincerely that every man has consummate genius within him. Some appear to have it more than others only because they are aware of it more than others are, and the awareness or unawareness of it is what makes each one of them into masters or holds them down to mediocrity.... Successful men grow more brilliant as they grow older.... Great men's lives begin at forty, where the mediocre man's life ends.

Naturally, Russell's message, transcribed well over seventy years ago by Glenn Clark in *The Man Who Tapped the Secrets of the Universe*, applies to women, too. Like Neville, Napoleon Hill, and other early icons of the human potential movement, Russell identifies the willingness to think and act constructively from a burning desire as the factor which determines mediocrity or genius—the latter quality is "self-bestowed."

The belief that we are, indeed, the creators of our reality brings me back to the advice that you can learn to use your imagination to become who you truly desire to be—in Neville's words, to "make your future dream a present fact." He writes, "You do this by assuming the feeling of your wish fulfilled." If, through a confident and steady will, you develop the ability to make your dominant feeling that of *already* living your dream, "the attainment of the ideal is inevitable."

Trust the Power of the Work Itself

Be who you are. Invent your own model of the life you'd love to live authentically and creatively, and learn all you can in order to make it work—including making your creative work known to others (that is, if you desire it to be known). Don't fear or be repulsed by promoting what you do. People in the arts often bring cynical attitudes to the table when it comes to marketing, advertising, social media, and the like. In most cases, artists want to be promoted: they just don't feel comfortable doing promotion for themselves. In part, undoubtedly, it's because of the time involved. Time is precious to all of us. Much creative time is often required for our work itself, whatever that work may be; it can be a stretch to consider self-promotion as a separate yet integral part of one's farther-reaching creative process.

I think another core reason is discomfort about blowing one's own horn. Many of us have ingrained negative messaging on the subject of self-promotion. Growing up, we may have been directed to stay quiet about our gifts and achievements; we've been conditioned to believe that making them well known would be bragging—somehow selfish and morally wrong. Many talented, creative people feel like imposters when it comes to sharing what they do, but the solution does not lie in hiding. Listen to the boldness in a robin's morning song and feel the beauty in that: no self-conscious trappings, no fakery. The bird simply relays its gifts for all to hear. Ask yourself, "What is my dream?" If it is to have your work be known, then I encourage you to be like the robin and release any negative messages you have internalized around letting your song be heard. Going forth in confidence is not the same as arrogance. In singing out confidently, you serve.

Strive in all you do to bring people value. A world that doesn't know about your gifts cannot receive them. If you sincerely have a contribution to make, then you must support yourself in making it. Don't succumb to lack of confidence or false modesty—both prevent making connections. It takes courage for many highly creative contributors to connect with the world. I love a statement that Maya Angelou made on that topic shortly before her death: "Courage," she said, "is the most important virtue because without it you can't uphold any of the others consistently." If you fear that advertising your creative work is boastful or selfish, remember that your creative acts are contributions, anchored in a sincere will to contribute meaningfully and authentically. Persist at what you love to do, and commit to taking action toward your creative dream of offering value to others.

If it helps you to get the message out about your work, remove yourself from the equation. Focus on the meaning and power of the work itself, and trust that you have been called to do what you do. Remind yourself of what your work contributes; consider how it addresses the needs and desires of your intended audience. The more you can recognize the novelty and usefulness of your work, the more you can feel confident in promoting it. Remember that any creative product or service is useful if it brings joy and enriches the life of another.

Will everyone love your work and find it valuable? Maybe, but probably not. That is good news, because it frees you. It is important to accept that you won't please everyone, even when authenticity, integrity and high levels of commitment and mastery are at the core of what you do. While you must not overlook your purpose in connecting meaningfully with readers, viewers, listeners, receivers, and fellow meaning-makers, you must also remain true to your vision and calling.

As a writer, and as someone who has artist friends who run the gamut of disciplines, I have heard just about every variation of a rejection story out there. After a while, rejections lose their sting. Take the gifts of each experience, and refuse entry to any beliefs or feelings that don't serve you. Move forward with an attitude of confidence and joy, feeling your wishes fulfilled, and persevere. Sometimes, after a work has been rejected not just several times but a great many, it suddenly meets with great success. We've all heard of examples. Perseverance is one of our most valuable assets, and the only one that makes a rejection-to-success story possible. Sometimes we discover that a work we've created has come through us to be our teacher, showing us the way and catalyzing the greater work that follows and is shared. Flexibility—the willingness to listen to what is required for growth and greater success—is also a vital asset. Use your intuition and feel where your desire is guiding you to focus. Occasionally a project returns for us to thank and release with love in the service of something greater still. Once again, persevere in your vision and in what you do.

"Do your work, and you shall reinforce yourself," Emerson reminds us. His words from the nineteenth century are still fresh. Doing your genuine work sometimes means accepting that while it will appeal to some, delivering worth and value, it may not and indeed probably won't appeal to everyone—not even everyone who is close to you.

Be who you are. If and when you take an arrow, even from the ones you love, gently remove it. Set it down. Keep moving positively, confidently, and authentically in the direction of your dream.

Creative Wellsprings: Fund Your Dream

Bless your income as energy that helps you to create and thrive. As a wise woman once reminded me, many artists and other consciously creative individuals abandon substantial income-earning positions in order to live authentically, only to quickly find that they're devoting most of their energy to scrambling for money.

You can hold one or more conventional jobs and still be authentically you. You can be a nonconformist in your ideas and creative life while earning money in tried and true ways to fund your dream. I devoted a good deal of my early adulthood to teaching in a traditional school, and school life gave back to me many times over. It was my learning laboratory for emergence as an artist and specialized coach, and prepared the way for my renewal at midlife. For many years before my career change, I had scheduled time, during summers and winter breaks, for writing—regardless of the outcome. For me, holidays spent writing truly *were* holidays. I love and live by Wayne Dyer's adage: "It's never crowded along the extra mile." Ask yourself how prepared you are to do the creative work you love. Where, in your calendar, are the extra miles? Schedule them. And don't forget to have fun! Know your priorities. Arrange your revenue-attracting activities to ensure that you have time to cultivate great health, creative passions, relationships, and joy.

Recently, I spoke with a dentist who became a mother in her forties. Now fifty, she has a well-established professional practice, as well as two young children and a husband who need her to play a vital role in their lives. She's also committed to writing a book. She gets up early each day, at 4:30 or 5:00 a.m., in order to write in this optimally creative time. This way, she stays on track without compromising the other ways she delivers value. Writing creatively gives her energy, and she is thriving.

None of us must be squeezed under the yoke of one career label. We are free to be multiple things at once. Throughout history we've seen many examples of prolific and significantly creative people with conventional day jobs. My favorite early example is Geoffrey Chaucer, who, in his fourteenth-century day, worked as a bureaucrat in the civil service, a courtier, and a diplomat. I love to imagine how his job must have supplied great material for *The Canterbury Tales*. I wonder if he wrote in the predawn hours, or late into the evening by the light of a single lamp. T.S. Eliot worked at Lloyd's Bank in London while he wrote "The Wasteland." Poet Wallace Stevens and musician Charles Edward Ives both worked as insurance executives. I love the story I heard, many years ago, of how poet William Carlos Williams, a pediatrician, drafted poems on prescription pads—a practice which may in part account for his poems' brevity. He made each word matter.

When I was recently in Concord, Massachusetts, I was struck by what a jack-of-all-trades Henry David Thoreau was: a surveyor at Walden Pond, a gardener, and a local handyman. I paused over a little desk which he was reputed to have built for Nathaniel Hawthorne. Hawthorne himself worked at conventional jobs in order to fund his lifelong dream of writing. He worked at Salem's Customs House, which still stands, as does much of the town of his era. It wasn't until he felt compelled to take that day job that Hawthorne produced his most important writing. The limitations of a busy schedule helped to galvanize his efforts, spurring him to make great use of whatever writing time he had. One of my favorite experiences while visiting Salem was sitting on the steps of the old Customs House, reading Hawthorne's description of it in the opening pages of *The Scarlet Letter*.

I derive inspiration from the story of P.D. James, who didn't come into her power as a writer until midlife. Forced to leave school at sixteen, she married an army doctor, who returned from World War II in ill health. James studied hospital administration and eventually took a position as a civil servant with the criminal section of the Home Office in order to support her family. It goes without saying that her work life informed her writing. She managed for many years to write murder mysteries while maintaining her position as a civil servant.

Obviously, these examples are just several of the many cases of prolific and talented creative people who funded their dreams by working other jobs, some with high demands and a public face. I recommend learning how to establish multiple sources of income to help you boost your sense of security and confidence in getting your creative work out into the world.

Be who you are. Let your day job(s) serve you and your dream, and let every job you do be a meaningful contribution. It's important to find balance and harmony in the whole picture. If you are starved for creative time, assess your situation: ask yourself what it would take to free up two extra hours a day for your creative pursuit. Then be flexible and willing to make sacrifices in doing what is necessary. In researching the routines of some of history's great artists in a variety of fields, I have discovered that many did not actively create for more than two or three hours a day, usually in the morning. I return to the teachings of the twentieth-century creator Walter Russell, a man whom news anchor Walter Cronkite referred to as "the Leonardo da Vinci of our time" for his contributions as a painter, sculptor, musician, equestrian, figure skater, metaphysician, and natural philosopher. He stayed in a constant flow of creative energy by working with single-pointed focus, and—here is the crucial point—by changing the subject of his focus every two hours. In that way, he professed, he was able to live multiple creative lives.

We all fulfill many roles. To live fully and authentically, you can keep your creative focus while providing service in ways which serve others and your dream—ways which make you the one and only you.

Territory

The robin is a bird that sings to mark its territory. Traditionally, as human beings, we have thought in terms of competing for ground—often quite literally, as in our wars. I choose to believe we are outgrowing that model. As individuals, each of us can make a decision to define "territory" with our authenticity and sincere intent to contribute well to a rich and sustainable world. Trust that you already have your territory by virtue of who you are, what you do, and all the creative ways you give value. Your territory is yours by virtue of who you are ever becoming. The very presence and life within you, seeking growth and expression, is freely given. You don't need to compete for this; you already have it. Trust that your ingenuity, sincere intent, and strong efforts to create meaningfully are all you need to succeed. People seek genuine connection. You being you, in your work and in your life, invites that connection.

Sing your song.

Claiming the Robin's Gift: Authenticity

Exercise 1: A Fond Look Back from the Future

List the highlights of a speech to be read at your own memorial service. What would you love to have accomplished in this beautiful incarnation once it's time, at long last, to go home? Consider all the important spheres of your life: your family and friends; your creative gifts and contributions; your altruism; your sense of fun, adventure, personal growth, and play; your shining spirit. This is not meant to be a morbid experience, but a clarifying and uplifting one! Alternatively, you may wish to write highlights from a speech someone gives at your 100th birthday party. You decide on the version which brings a sense of elation that comes in fulfilling a mission.

Have you updated your bucket list lately? If not, start this exercise by making a list of fifty things you'd love to do while passing through this world. This will give you some of the material for your speech highlights.

Exercise 2: Your Life Mission Statement

Reflecting on all that you have written, visualized, and done so far in service of your creative growth, what do you feel is your mission in this lifetime? Write a mission statement for your life. In the spirit of self-discovery and growth, your statement can be modified at any time.

As in Exercise 1, consider all of the domains of your life and assess how well your day-to-day situation supports the fulfillment of your mission. Are there changes you can make that will increase that support? The clearer your sense of mission, the more you will be clear about taking action to fulfill it. You may choose to type and frame your mission statement, placing it where you can see it each day as a galvanizing reminder. You may also wish to write yours on a wallet card and carry it with you. It's up to you.

Key Ideas

Which of these ideas would you like to be routinely reminded of? Copy any that cause you to feel inspired to take action and post them where you will see them regularly.

- Living authentically is acting in alignment with core values and a sense of mission. Finding what you love is about finding who you truly are. The clearer your sense of mission, the better able you will be to withstand any challenges which may arise on the creative path.
- Childhood memories can help us to reconnect with our unique and innate sense of mission. Relish the "humdrum miracles" in your past. You can only connect the dots of experience by looking backward; in memory, learn to recognize the signposts of your calling and authenticity.
- Regardless of your current circumstances, you can both love and live your aim.
- Imagination is your superpower: it holds the key to keeping you on track to creative fulfillment.

- Cultivating a beginner's mind is a key element in mastery.
- Common denominators in the personalities of creative high achievers include motivation and a willingness to go the extra mile.
- "The very cave you are afraid to enter turns out to be the source of what you are looking for." —Joseph Campbell
- That part of you which seeks expansion—your pure creativity—is ageless.
- When you learn to make your future dream a present fact, assuming the feeling of the wish fulfilled, you and your positive actions become a magnet for your dream.
- Any creative product or service which brings joy, and in any way enriches the life of another, is useful.
- Trust the power of the work you feel called to do. Make your gifts known.
- You are free to play multiple roles. Bless your income as the energy that sustains your creative life.
- Where are your extra miles? Schedule them.
- What would it take to free up two extra hours a day for your creative pursuit?
- Cultivate and trust your authenticity, knowing that you are a creative being whose presence and work makes the world a better place.

Chapter 4
The Crow and the Raven: Freeing Your Vision, Intuition, and Action

I dream with silvery gull
And brazen crow.
A thing that is beautiful
I may know.
—Patrick Kavanagh

One Book

A dozen years ago, one of my English-teaching colleagues, Dee, took me aside after a meeting. She gestured to my journal, where I'd just taken copious notes. "Is that where you do all your writing?" she asked. In addition to being an accomplished teacher, my colleague was also an essayist and poet intent upon seeing more of her work published. Like me, Dee wrote on the edges of her day job.

At first I was surprised by her question. I'd kept a journal for many years and the book had become as normal for me to carry as my wallet, phone, lipstick and compact, subway pass, and reading material. (Yes, I have a big purse.) The fact that she took an interest in my journal startled me.

I nodded.

"Then that's your secret," said Dee. "You only use one book."

"Uh-huh."

Dog-eared, coffee-splattered, with Post-it notes peeking past the edges: one book.

She was visibly pleased by the "ah-ha" (or, rather, "uh-huh") moment. As I tucked my silent, spiral-bound companion back into the portable cavern on my shoulder, she added, "That's so much better than dividing things up—notebooks for school, books for drafting, books for journaling, grocery lists, etc. To carry it all in one book makes sense. Then you always have it ready." When I heard those words, it suddenly occurred to me that in fact I'd done much to arrive at a simple system that worked. I'd made journaling ordinary—so ordinary, in fact, that I'd forgotten all that had gone into establishing my own habit and system. My friend found magic in my ordinary: one book for everything.

This chapter is about exploring various creative uses for your one essential notebook—that is, beyond the daily practice outlined in Chapter 2. (We will not be discussing grocery lists, though like me you may wish to write them in your notebook, too!) Expect each of your journals to look more than gently loved by the time you're finished filling it. I recommend using a book that feels right to you. Sometimes rough and ready is best: a drugstore purchase or a dollar-store find, a book you don't mind scribbling in. If you carry a "precious keepsake" journal—something hard-covered, expensive, and aesthetically pleasing—then by all means scribble in that, too! Never be daunted by the appearance, cost, or quality of the book you write in. Treasure comes in many forms. Make carrying your book part of your everyday, ordinary magic.

Black Feather

To me, the bird that most readily signals magic in the ordinary is the common crow. How many times have you stopped to locate its lusty caw? Have you felt awe in beholding those blue-black wings flapping and twitching atop a power pole, or swooping down to a ditch in which the bird then deftly feasts? Have you ever gasped in wonder (or even, perhaps, shivered) to find a perfect black feather in the grass? Picking and strutting, the crow reminds us that real treasure exists in the everyday world.

Alas, in recent centuries in the West, these intelligent and highly social creatures have had a bad rap. Some have considered crows and ravens unsettling pests or, worse, portents of doom. Carrion eaters, these edgiest members of the Corvidae family, were associated with death in days when European ancestors caught them dining on dead livestock, or plucking the eyeballs from slain soldiers strewn on battlefields. In Shakespeare's time, the birds were considered to be evil harbingers of death. *Macbeth*, the classic study of murder and its bloody consequences, is a drama rife with black-winged augurs. Edgar Allan Poe didn't like the birds, either; his poem "The Raven" helped to make the crow's big cousin into the original goth totem—an icon of gloom. In her 1995 book *Bird Brains*, Candace Savage recounts that as recently as 1989, "members of the British House of Lords rose in outrage against the suggestion that they [crows] be protected by law." She goes on to state that in North America, "in many rural areas, taking potshots at magpies and crows is still seen as a respectable pastime—indeed a public service." A defender of corvids, and a well-studied, persuasive enthusiast, Savage ably supports the claim that crows and ravens are sensitive, skilled, and complex creatures deserving of human respect and protection.

In fact, throughout history and across cultures, more often than not, crows and ravens *have* been respected—even revered. In her engaging work *Ravensong*, author Catherine Feher-Elston places these birds in a much older, broader, and more spiritual context: "Many European societies once honored the Raven, the Earth Mother, and all of the natural powers those entities represented. Ravens and crows were believed to be omniscient, to know all things past, present, and to come." She cites various cultures that regarded the birds as emblems of wisdom, magic, medicine, and leadership. Feher-Elston writes, "It is said that Odin, father of the Norse and Teutonic gods, was accompanied in his travels by two ravens, Thought and Memory; he sent them out to survey the world each morning, and instructed them to bring back all the news to him." She goes on to point out that almost all Native peoples of the Americas have viewed crows and ravens as mysterious, mischievous, and sacred tricksters, "shamanic... associated with healing, magic and successful hunting." Native peoples of both the east and west coasts have associated these birds with divinity. "They are almost always considered to be messengers between the living and the spirit worlds," writes Feher-Elston. Perhaps that's why, to this day, many feel crows put us in touch with our intuition.

And our creativity.

The Crow: Master Caller and Collector

The crow's black wings remind us that all creation begins in the dark. Its voice: a signal to live boldly. This bird doesn't have just one call, but many—"an incredible range of vocalization" as Feher-Elston notes, and as Savage affirms in her account of being alternately barked at and trilled to by the same cocked-headed corvid. Ted Andrews likens the crow's sound to "the secret magic of creation calling." A keen observer, this animal also has a sharp eye for detail; a consummate collector, it sees what shines and claims it. I invite you to remember the crow's two great gifts as you read and work through this chapter: 1) the ability to call in different ways for different purposes and 2) the propensity to gather all that's needed for nourishment and skillful building.

May your creativity be nourished and your building be inspired, skillful, and meaningful. In Chapter 2, I urged you to write freely each morning, allowing thoughts which naturally arise to find expression on your page. I now also strongly encourage you to use your journal for much more; below I outline several "calls" and answers available to you through your journal practice. You can benefit immensely by employing these techniques. While the calls in this section can be done any time and in any order, the call to vision is a powerful, natural first.

The Call to Vision

In this practice, "vision" is an action word—not just a noun but also a verb. I like to vision in a semi-meditative state. The role of meditation in creativity is one of the key subjects of Chapter 7; for now, suffice it to say that when we learn to meditate for prolonged periods of time, we shift our brain-wave frequency from beta to alpha. In so doing, we have a great opportunity to embed ideas in the subconscious mind. As discussed in Chapters 1 and 2, the subconscious is where our prevailing thoughts, feelings, and beliefs reside; it perpetuates our paradigm. In a quiet, meditative, alpha-wave state, we can choose the ideas we think about; what's more, we can learn to impress upon the subconscious mind a vision of our choosing.

The more we bring our five senses to imaginative visioning, and the more charged with positive emotion that experience is, the better able we are, over time and with consistent practice, to effect changes in the subconscious mind. In the *Dhammapada*, the Buddha says, "With our thoughts we create the world." Thoughts, as dendrite connections formed by brain cells, really do manifest as physical structures. They also function as invisible creative agents. When thoughts and actions align with vision, intention becomes a powerful magnet.

I invite you to experiment with visioning. Spend five minutes sitting in quiet meditation each night before bed. (If nothing else, doing so will probably help you get to sleep!) One night, start early enough that, instead of turning out the light after meditating, you can spend the next twenty minutes visualizing a desired experience. Make the experience as real as you can with your senses. Here are three very brief examples of visioning. Each can be adapted and expanded upon:

- If you're composing a film score, imagine details of the opening night gala. Who is with you? How do you feel? See your name roll in the credits, and watch as the director turns and smiles at

you. Feel the plush seat. Smell the popcorn. Hear the music and applause. Afterward, listen to people discussing the strengths of the film, including its gorgeous music. "Who wrote it?" "How glorious." Know, even without hearing others' compliments, that your work adds beauty to the world. Now how do you feel?
- If you're creating a vibrant, magnetic website, really see it. Feel the pleasure of being captivated by your chosen visuals, design, and menu. Enjoy the experience of seeing your e-mail list grow as people respond positively to your offerings, because your gifts make a beautiful difference to them. Can you picture their positive messages? Can you hear them speaking with you on the phone?
- If you're planning to mount an art show, create the gallery opening in your mind: the sound of conversations as viewers behold your assemblages and paintings, the gasps of wonder, the clicks of people's heels on the wooden floor. Taste the sparkling water in your glass, the cheese and fruit, the fancy crackers. Visualize the red dots beside your art work that indicate sales and the checks the gallery owner hands you. Imagine how it feels to earn money doing what you love best.

Whatever your vision is, pay no attention to the "how" of getting there from your present circumstance, only to the "what." Do the exercise until you feel as positively as you can. Sometimes your enthusiasm will be mild at best; other times, you will feel it build as you make kinesthetic, visual, and auditory connections. Open your journal and write down the details of your experience as you've just lived it. Use the present tense, as the subconscious mind knows only *now*.

Unlike your morning freewriting experiences, for this exercise, choose your words carefully as you record your vision, further impressing the details upon your subconscious mind. Note that if you say "I *want* this," you merely perpetuate wanting. Instead, give thanks that you *already have* the desired state or thing, and be grateful. Recall the powerful directive to live from the dream.

You may also wish to create present-tense affirmations, worded in positive terms, out of the visioning experience and repeat them to yourself. Better yet, record your affirmations, so that you're in the alpha state when you play back your own words. Crafting affirmative self-talk is a learned skill; in my coaching practice, I find that many of my clients benefit greatly from help in growing their abilities in this area. You can make an excellent start by beginning each statement with gratitude: "I am so happy and grateful now that...."

Enjoy the ways your vision serves not only you but others. Look for the gifts. Set your vision in the future—two, three, or five years away—and see the details unfold as though they are already memories. Just as you listen to your recorded affirmations daily, after writing your vision statement, I encourage you to read it aloud, with emotion, several times each day, bringing positive images, ideas, and feelings to the experience.

Respect your creative goals and dreams by letting them gestate in the dark for a while. Keep your ideas confidential until you find the right person, preferably a trusted coach and/or mentor, to speak with. Don't share your vision with anyone who might, even with the best of intentions, criticize it or try to talk you out of it. Sometimes the people who are closest to us are the ones most likely to discourage us, out of fear, from following our dreams. For now, keep your dream to yourself as you fly on the beautiful wings of your vision.

Active visioning is the expansive and disciplined work of the imagination, our most powerful technology. Learn to nurture and respect your mind as a divine center of creation.

The Call to Question

I've heard it said many times over that art is a series of problems to solve. When facing a creative challenge, I've learned to turn to my journal to get results. In this section, I hope to help you to do the same. The call to question moves us from constructive thinking into action and, ultimately, solution. This call can take various forms. The techniques I use most often are brainstorming, conducting an inner-wisdom dialogue, and a combination of the two.

The brainstorming technique is simple, requiring only your journal, a pen, a good question, and the willingness to be open-minded in accessing wisdom from a higher power. (As in earlier exercises, use your chosen name for that power; call it your higher self, if you like.) In this activity, allow for fresh and surprising possibilities as you cultivate intuition. (Remember the crow's bold call!) The wonderful thing about this practice is that you need not pay to consult an outside specialist in order to find answers to your questions; you already have that specialist within. What's more, you can learn to channel the voice of inner guidance quite readily in your journal, and at a moment's notice.

When brainstorming to find answers, it's important to ask good questions. I've learned much on the subject of forming strongly generative questions from my teacher, Mary Morrissey, who is an international speaker, a visionary, and an empowerment specialist. She cites Einstein, who was once asked what he'd do if he had only an hour to solve a difficult problem. He replied that he would spend the first 55 minutes determining the proper question to ask... for once he knew the proper question, he could solve the problem in less than five minutes. Einstein also said that we can't solve problems by using the same kind of thinking we used when we created them. Forming the right question is crucial because it takes us to a new and higher level. Mary emphasizes that the solution to a problem always exists on the same vibrational frequency as the proper question. Her work has been pivotal in my life, showing me that for every conceivable problem there *is* a conceivable solution. Forming great questions and accessing intuition are important keys to creative growth. It's no wonder Mary calls brainstorming "sourcing."

In my study of human potential, I've learned that when initiating a search for answers it's best to begin your question with the word "what" rather than "how," "when," or "why." "What" questions are richly generative because they connect us with action; it's important when we seek guidance that we're prepared not only to receive information but to act on it in the service of a creative vision. "What steps can I take?" "What can I do?" Those are good ways to begin a line of questioning. What actions can you take to live in alignment with the dream that calls you? Allow yourself to receive a full brainstorm of information and action steps. Even if your thoughts seem to dry up, keep going. I learned many years ago in teaching that when we brainstorm we often reach a point at which we stall; the best thing to do is wait it out.

When you brainstorm, don't judge your ideas as they flow onto the page. By allowing thoughts to emerge quickly and loosely, you circumvent your subconscious mind's tight hold and escape your limiting paradigm. The results can be revealing and expansive. If, as you write freely, you find negative, self-deprecating thoughts cropping up, know they're from the ego, that critic inside each of us. Thoughts of self-judgment which feel destructive are part of an old, internal program of learned beliefs. So are thoughts which feel forced, those "shoulds" that sound like the answers others would like to hear. When such thoughts intrude, learn to replace them with mental images of success. Then ask to reconnect with your own inner wisdom and transcend the mental chatter. Continue your brainstorming until you've generated a list of at least twenty-five ideas. Once you have your brainstormed list, you're ready to sort and select the ideas with the greatest charge—those which inspire you, even if they're daunting or downright scary. Letting your intuition take the lead, use your judgment constructively now as you let the other ideas go. Select only those few thoughts which move you to take authentic, constructive action. Prepare to schedule your follow-up steps.

As I mentioned earlier in this chapter in the opening of "The Call to Question," in addition to brainstorming, I also use my journal to dialogue with a voice of inner wisdom. This form of dialogue journaling begins, like brainstorming, with a good question. The difference is that the inner-wisdom dialogue technique is simply a natural, free flow of questions and answers. The writer literally has a discussion on the page with the higher self. I know a woman who opens such intuitive conversations with "Dear Beloved." In doing so, she gains clarity in decision making. Treat your own inner guidance system as beloved. Be grateful in all you do, regardless of your present circumstances; in accessing gratitude, you access the beloved in you. When you seek wise guidance from a higher power, the act of seeking in itself affirms you're on the right track.

The Call to Commune

Many years ago, in my undergrad days, I met a young man in the University of Toronto's Robarts Library stacks. Complete strangers, we struck up a conversation in a philosophy aisle of the building otherwise known in our city as Fort Book. As we mused together over the names and contributions of some of the great philosophers in history, he asked me who I'd invite to my own salon. Intrigued, and a little baffled, I asked him to explain. "Who would you choose," he said, "if you could call upon any of the great thinkers who've ever lived to be your own, private guests? Who would you like to learn from? What would you discuss?"

    I've never forgotten the sense of wonder and possibility in that brief encounter in the dim, dusty old stacks. I never saw the young man again, but I remembered his question two decades later when I discovered the work of Napoleon Hill. Since that discovery, Hill's most famous book, *Think and Grow Rich*, is one I've turned to many times for inspiration and clarity. Many synchronistic events have pointed me back to that book. Near the end, Hill provides instructions for creating a private council of "Wise Guides" to consult when guidance is required, regardless of whether the members of the council are living or dead. Obviously, this exercise requires the power of imagination as well as what the poet Samuel Taylor Coleridge called "the willing suspension of disbelief." I recommend reading (and rereading) Hill's work, and using the Wise Guides exercise as a variation of inner-wisdom journaling.

I see this call as an act of communion—not only with kindred spirits but with your core being. The very act of choosing your Wise Guides can reveal much about you, your dreams and inspirations, your questions, and your willingness to take action in the service of a burning desire. Who are your role models? What do you choose to learn from them?

When I work with the journal in this way, writing down received insights and advice, I appreciate, on a deeper level, just what Einstein meant when he said that imagination is greater than knowledge. But it doesn't have to be "either/or"; with this exercise, we nurture and develop both.

The Call to Gather and Inspire

In my life, writing and spiritual questing have been inseparable. No matter the form—poetry, fiction, nonfiction, article or blog—at core, I'm reflecting on the nature of embodied life on this place we call earth. In the fiction I write, my characters are questing characters. The border between exploring our spiritual nature through writing and through reading has always been very thin for me. Sometimes, on the surface, what I'm reading appears to be vastly different from my current writing project, yet I know that each experience informs the other. I'm ever scribbling in the margins of what I've read, transferring gifts of insight.

The crow is a consummate collector, drawn to what shines. What artists' messages shine for you? I encourage you to write them down. Collect them in your journal. One problem with using a computer for written communication is that the "copy and paste" and "share" features of our wired world require almost no time or kinesthetic effort on our part. We grab information quickly and save it to myriad files on the desktop, e-mail it, post it on Facebook, tweet it—send it to whatever digital hidey-holes we can think of—and it promptly disappears from view. When we take the time to write out the words of the thinkers we revere, we experience their rhythms and meanings, not only visually, but kinesthetically. (And those of us who "hear" words in our heads as we write will experience them auditorily as well.) We have a record, in our own hand, of meeting a fellow artist on life's pages. We also have a record of the context, when we see our own thoughts scrawled around the entry—even if our next entry is (ahem…) a grocery list.

An English teacher I knew spent a good deal of time working to memorize poems and passages she loved, claiming them as part of the fabric of her experience. She recited Shakespeare and Milton on the way to the corner variety store, and Mary Oliver while waiting for the dentist. Why not? On one visit to Northern Ireland, I wrote out a poem by Patrick Kavanagh in my journal and carried it with me, attempting to recall and recite these lines as I walked the Armagh fields:

Ploughman

I turn the lea-green down
Gaily now,
And paint the meadow brown
With my plough.

I dream with silvery gull
And brazen crow.
A thing that is beautiful
I may know.

Tranquility walks with me
And no care.
O, the quiet ecstasy
Like a prayer.

> I find a star-lovely art
> In a dark sod.
> Joy that is timeless! O heart
> That knows God!

Serendipitous now, as I draft this chapter, is the crow in Kavanagh's poem. I'd forgotten that kindred, dreaming—and, yes, brazen!—presence. And so it goes: this star-lovely, ordinary, extraordinary life.

What are you reading these days? What websites, blog posts, boards, walls, and e-mails? What signs? What books? What pictures, films and dances are you experiencing? Take time to jot down wisdom in whatever form it comes. Like the crow, ever reading the world, find what shines for you and claim it. Make it part of your story.

The Call to Create: Scheduling, Planning, and Drafting

Crows are not impulsive birds; they may be daring, but their moves are intelligent. Recall Aesop's fable of the thirsty crow that wants to sip water from the bottom of a pitcher, beyond its beak's reach. The crow drops pebbles into the pitcher one by one until the water finally rises high enough for the creature to drink. Similarly, although the visions to which we aspire can appear beyond our reach, we can, like the undaunted, resourceful crow, choose to employ strategy and discipline to attain them. Indeed, to be successful in our quest, we must do so. Ingenuity, planning, and follow-through are crucial traits of all dreamers who dare to see their visions manifest.

The importance of acting in the service of your creative vision cannot be overemphasized. All the free-writing, meditating, visioning, questioning, communing, reading, and gathering of inspiration are intrinsically valuable; but without action, you'll likely stay where you are: dreaming. If you truly aim to see your vision manifest, focused action *must* occur in addition to those foundational practices. Yes, taking action can be scary. But remember all the ways you're growing! Your steps need not be big, they need only *be*. Take them — even if you're afraid. Call upon your trust and faith to set some creative wheels in motion. Each time you push through your fears, you'll be surprised at the way they shrink as your confidence grows. While taking small steps, you can still think big. In fact, why not think very big? Your mind is free. All the while, keep moving forward.

The best way to ensure that you take constructive action is to create a schedule and follow it. If we're to advance confidently, we must schedule in the direction of our dreams and follow our plans. Use your journal to help you make a plan at the beginning of each day, week, month, and year. Planning and follow-through are as crucial to fulfilling a burning desire as the desire itself.

Schedule small, measurable and achievable moves, just as the crow dropped one stone at a time into the beaker. I recommend limiting your goals to sets of three, especially if your days are very full. Choose three goals for each day, week, month, and year. (Unless you're experiencing an unusually busy stretch, don't count your morning journal practice, or your visioning work and affirmation statements. They're a given.) In every busy day, be sure that *one* of your three primary goals serves your creative vision. Remember to give yourself wins — each time you achieve even the smallest goal in the direction of your dream, note it down and celebrate. I like to use a large wall calendar and plan in three- and six-month increments, as well as one-year and three-year blocks. In whatever way works for you, plan. Learn to reliably give yourself a command and follow through. I once received valuable advice to stop using the word "try." Shift from trying to doing. Make manageable plans and follow through.

The Call to Collect and Organize

I return to this chapter's opening idea that using one book for all pen-to-paper writing is an efficient and powerful catalyst for creativity. Again, I encourage you to use your journal to rough out and house whatever thoughts, plans, and creative enterprises are emerging. All of my fiction, nonfiction, poetry, blogs and other project drafts find expression in my journal before I type. So do my morning free-writes, dreams and visions, questions, brainstorms and inner-wisdom dialogues, responses to reading and inspirational quotes, schedule notes, and, of course, to-do lists and other miscellaneous daily jottings. If your primary mode of creative expression isn't writing, you can still use your journal very fruitfully in the service of your projects. Here are a few suggestions; adapt them as you see fit:

- If you're an artist in any visual medium, a sketchbook without lines makes the best journal of all. I often switch to blank books with luxuriously thick paper just to feel a spaciousness in my process. Sometimes I sketch; always I scrawl in pace with my thoughts. Such a journal does not become a showpiece—and that's the point. By staying loose and allowing rough work to take form, you open the way for many future showpieces.
- If you're a musician, you can create customized journals cheaply at a local printing shop, combining blank pages for writing along with staff paper for composing. You may also consider gluing staff paper into a sturdy bound book for use on an as-needed basis. Either way, you have a ready-made, contained place for rough work.
- I encourage you to incorporate found images into your journal. From magazines and the Internet, choose pictures that inspire you and help to clarify your goals and dreams. Search for logos, ad copy, photos of interior and exterior spaces—anything relevant—to spark your creativity. While this practice is especially useful for entrepreneurs beginning a new creative venture, I encourage people in all walks of life to collect images for inspiration.

Paradoxically, while for the best results we must allow ourselves to create freely and even messily, we must be systematic and organized in our approach to storing work—highlighting, flagging, and labelling what we've created—so we can have access to it as needed. (One key difference between a crow and a magpie is that the crow keeps a tidier nest.)

The remainder of this short section is on the joy and effective use of office supplies and systems. The aim here is to help you cultivate habits that empower you, so you'll know what you have and where it is. Joy is an empowering emotion. For me, an experience which readily brings joy is shopping for office supplies! I feel like a little kid when I get to choose my "toys"—and with an adult's budget, the thrills come relatively cheaply. Here's a list of suggested supplies to help you feel rich in your creative nest:

- Journals—These can be either cheap and cheerful or fancy; use whatever feels right for you.
- Fast-moving pens—If you use a fountain pen, then have cartridges or an inkwell at the ready.
- Highlighter pens—Get a range of different colors. I recommend the kind that won't smear your ink.
- Sticky labels—Use these for labeling the front covers of your journals with the dates they cover.
- Post-it notes—These are essential for flagging key pages.
- Storage bins—Get airtight ones to guard against flooding. One bin will hold several years' worth of your journals.
- Computer—Even if you create rough drafts by hand, you'll eventually want to type and store some documents.
- Printer—Important pages need to be typed, printed, and filed.
- Paper—Be sure to stock up!
- File folders and file hangers—Make sure you have so many that

you won't be afraid to make mistakes in how you file things.
- File cabinet—Alternatively, you can find containers designed to take file hangers.

Invest in making both your creative workspace and the work itself organized. Because I'm a person who uses one book for everything, it's essential that I review my journals before placing them in the bins. I need to look back at what I've written each week and month. I create a color key for highlighting various categories, including drafts, notes, words of wisdom gleaned from reading, and so on. Usually I limit to four or five color categories, or it's too confusing.

Remember that the crow is a consummate collector! Look for what catches your eye and code it. Emerson called his journal his "savings bank," and he spent a great deal of time rereading, reflecting upon and revising his rough material. Eventually, through long and passionate effort, the entries he "saved" evolved into erudite, profound and poetic essays, many of which still resonate today. For a modern journaling "collector," it's important to commit time, routinely, to typing up work that needs saving in computer files. As I was beginning to write this book, I had the uncanny experience of discovering a treasure trove of unfinished poems I'd jotted, typed, and filed in 2006. Back then, I was writing on spring ravine walks in my old neighborhood; serendipitously, those old poems, while unfinished and in need of further revision, felt completely fresh and aligned with my current experience. Because the old pieces had been typed and filed, I suddenly had a great stash of material for jump-starting current writing. Natalie Goldberg writes about "composting" material, and how it's crucial sometimes to save rough writing for years before revising. Life's raw material doesn't always yield its richest meaning until time passes.

Date your journal entries and the journals themselves, so you know where to find old material which may, surprisingly or not, become relevant again. This happened to me recently when an editor asked me to describe a particular setting in greater detail in my nineteenth-century novel. I needed to open the bin and find my journal from years before. I found interview notes I'd taken and was able to reconnect with an expert, then rewrite the relevant section with greater accuracy and effect. The process of going back and reconnecting caused new details to emerge in my revision—some unexpected turns that kept my story fresh and alive for me.

Adapt the process to whatever creative path and pursuit you're on. Ask yourself what you might need to find someday. Being organized is the key to making the most of your own creative genius.

The Raven

This story of Crow's big cousin comes from the Pacific Northwest Coast, where the Native peoples of North America have a long tradition of honoring Raven as a divine light-bearer, holy trickster, and emblem of transformation. For the early inhabitants of Beringia, Raven didn't come down the coast, as the indigenous people once had, but had always been there—a magic and powerful creator. According to Haida myth, Raven grew restless with the light-filled world he'd made. Canadian artist Bill Reid and cultural historian Robert Bringhurst recount the tale in "The Raven and the First Men":

> He [Raven] gave a great sigh, crossed his wings behind his back and walked along the sand, his shiny head cocked, his sharp eyes and ears alert for any unusual sight or sound. Then taking to the air, he called petulantly out to the empty sky. To his delight, he heard an answering cry—or to describe it more closely, a muffled squeak.
>
> At first he saw nothing, but as he scanned the beach again, a white flash caught his eye, and when he landed

he found at his feet, half buried in the sand, a gigantic clam shell. When he looked more closely still, he saw that the shell was full of little creatures cowering in terror of his enormous shadow....

But nothing was going to happen as long as the tiny things stayed in the shell, and they certainly weren't coming out in their present terrified state. So the Raven leaned his great head close to the shell, and with the smooth trickster's tongue that had got him into and out of so many misadventures...he coaxed and cajoled and coerced the little creatures to come out and play in his wonderful, shiny new world.

This myth serves as an allegory for the creative process. Each of us, a being of great power, calls out to a seemingly empty sky. So often we glide on the dark wings of restlessness, yearning, and creative potential, searching the world we've made for inspiration. Then something catches the eye—a flash! a gleam!—a body of thought, beckoning, like that clam shell. In the books we've filled, we discover our own ideas calling us back to find them: an entire creative populace just waiting to be coaxed forth. "But nothing was going to happen as long as the tiny things stayed in the shell...." I love this moment of tension in the process, when the divine bird must reassure the shell's inhabitants to step forward. They cower in the creator's shadow as our own dreams do, timid creatures who must be loved into the light of realization.

We are the creators and the created, the seekers, the finders and the found. Each of us must become that beautiful trickster, coaxing our own "first thoughts" into the light of consciousness and our own faith that we can transform what begins as a "muffled squeak" into a work of art.

Key Ideas

As usual, review the statements below. Choose three to five which particularly resonate and, where appropriate, rewrite them as affirmations. Add them to your growing collection. Now find some inspirational pictures to post along with your affirmations in your creative space.

- One very ordinary journal equals magic.
- Treasure comes in many forms.
- Creation naturally begins in the dark.
- You have the ability to call for, and gather, all that's needed for your own creative growth and journey.
- "Vision" is an active verb.
- When positive thoughts, emotions and actions align with vision, intention becomes a powerful magnet.
- Whatever your vision is, pay no attention to the "how" of getting there from your present circumstance, only to the "what"—the details of your creative dream. Trust that with faith, practice, and constructive actions, the "how" always reveals itself.
- Write affirmations in the present tense; the subconscious mind only knows *now*.
- When brainstorming to find answers, it's important to ask good questions. Beginning a question with "What" can be richly generative, as such questions connect us with action.
- Let your ideas flow freely on the page.
- Treat your inner guidance system as beloved. Be grateful in all you do, regardless of your present circumstances; in accessing gratitude, you access the beloved in you.
- Who are your role models? What messages inspire and enrich you? Attract and collect those messages—and act on them.

- Schedule to make small, measurable and achievable moves. Each time you meet even the smallest goal in the direction of your dream, note it down and give yourself a win.
- Shift from trying to doing. Make your plans manageable, then follow through.
- Creativity is messy. Yet, as poet Alexander Pope reminds us, "Order is heaven's first law." Live the paradox! Write freely, but take an organized approach to highlighting, flagging, typing and storing your rough work.
- Like Crow and Raven, ever reading the world, find what shines for you and claim it. Make it part of your story.

Chapter 5
The Duck: Freeing Your Emotions and Discernment

No tears in the writer, no tears in the reader.
No surprise in the writer, no surprise in the reader.
—Robert Frost

A Walk in the Sand

At first I saw only feathers. When I pulled, I found them lodged somehow and I pulled harder. It took me several seconds to realize they belonged to an almost intact body buried in the sand. Then up came the bird's carcass, complete but for a cleanly severed head. I bagged the animal's remains and continued walking, the weight a welcome mystery.

Back at the workshop I showed Lana, an artist and intuitive healer, who was facilitating our session on reading found objects and incorporating nature's messages in art. She identified my bird as a duck.

A duck. I confess, I was a little crestfallen that the harbinger I'd claimed and come to consult on wasn't more edgy and arresting, like a cormorant or hawk or, even better, an eagle. Yes! To return from the Toronto Islands with an *eagle* in my big orange bag—now *that* would have been a kick-ass auger. A duck, on the other hand, made me think of Hans Christian Andersen's story of an ugly, misunderstood creature, an outsider who endures disconnection, yearning, and painful constrictions only to realize its full identity as nothing less than a magnificent swan. Read: *Not a duck.* My ego wanted something bigger.

I thought of duck feet and adjusted my stance. I thought of Daffy

Duck, and of Donald and Daisy quacking, and cleared my throat. Of course my ego, disappointed by the synchronicity I'd experienced on the beach, was the same ego that didn't reveal to my friend I was disappointed. "Ah… a duck," I said, like I'd found gold or a sacred chalice.

Quack, quack.

Yet as I handled the animal's body, stroking its feathers and fanning its wings, studying the curled feet, all of my mind's cartoon antics vanished.

"They may not fly very high, but they sure know how to dive," said Lana.

Of course. All at once it became clear that the webbing and wings were for a different medium altogether.

"Emotion," I said. "Deep water."

Suddenly I understood why the animal and I had found each other. I knew my job that summer would be to dive deeply into the interior life of my current novel's protagonist. I also knew the work would require me to plumb my own emotional depths; to say that I felt daunted was an understatement.

Months earlier, I thought I'd already gone deep enough in producing a manuscript that had been praised and circulated. But prospective publishers wanted more access to my central character's inner wounds. When I received their comments I wanted to shout, "Don't you know he's emotionally shut down? Isn't it obvious that his feelings are buried—so buried that even *he* can't feel them?!"

The inherent contradiction in my unvoiced defense had caused me to step back from the project all spring. I'd waited for the school year to end, knowing I'd need space to remember and explore how an emotionally damaged person feels and doesn't feel—how feelings come out sideways, and how to show that.

The duck's head was gone, yet it spoke. Don't bother searching for answers in your head, it said. Dive down.

Diving

The challenge: to go back again into the dive, the murk, the pain and wonder of the created world without questioning why I conceived of it in the first place, accepting that it came for a reason and the reason was a mystery—accepting that this was my child, my creation, and that even though it was June and sunny and people were happily sipping coffee on café patios and cycling in the ravines, I was in my basement in the dark of my character's transitory hell.

I'd spent the spring reading books on post-traumatic stress disorder in order to do justice to my novel's protagonist. I'd read other works on emotional pain and abandonment, and I'd made copious notes. I had internalized all I could through my researcher's brain—that safe place of being a learner, of material you can talk about at dinner parties when people ask you what you do. All the library books, e-books, articles, and bookmarked sites were conventional, appropriate, academic. But I knew what was coming: the propeller blade's clean swoop.

My heart, not my mind, would need to take the lead in those margins where the editor had written, "But what does he *feel*?"

The biggest obstacle in making the dive back into character work was my paradigm. I still experienced old, lingering shame and artistic self-doubt from years of negotiating deep-seated fears and "managing" my own emotions so well as to bury them—so deeply and seemingly completely that at times I feared true feelings had stopped existing in me. That fallacy was inextricable from my "failed actress who shouldn't have given up" narrative of myself. Eventually, through creative recovery work, I'd discovered I had hit a wall in acting when I couldn't quite "get" the feeling underlying the stage action. I understood motivation, but it was hard to access emotion in performance (that is, beyond a child's joy in play and the excitement of the adrenalin rush), because for me, emotion—and, more specifically, the vulnerability in intimately conveying emotion—was terrifying. I had ambition and stage presence, but I had a tough time *feeling* on cue. I was twenty-two.

Now, many years of recovery later, as a writer on the edge of facing what felt like the ultimate challenge, I worried I didn't have what it would take to find the emotional truth of my beloved character. Yet as much as I worried, I also recognized the ludicrousness of my fear. This story had moved me deeply from the start. Like every significant creative project in my life, it felt like a received work. My job was simply to bring the work into form—completely. I'd spent many an afternoon drafting outdoors, letting nature contain the story and my free-flowing tears in breakthrough moments when more was revealed to me. This summer would be no different. I felt a deep connection to my protagonist. I *knew* him. I simply had to trust my own emotional knowing, my range of experience and—yes—feelings, in order to access more of his.

I agree with Frost's sentiment, cited in this chapter's epigraph, that the poet's tears are the connective tissue of his work. Those tears need not be made obvious (indeed, our craft teachers remind us, "Show, don't tell"), yet the artist's emotion must translate to the cathartic experience of others as they view, read, explore, listen, dance: tears of sadness and also of laughter—of joy. Art is made through full-spectrum feeling in both the artist and the co-creative receiver. Regardless of the form our "poetry" takes, our range of emotion is its life force.

Left unchecked, my mind is very good at caging me with old stories of being so injured, defective, and "naturally" flawed as to not be capable of making fine art. Yours may be too. And there are variations of the cage story. Ask yourself if any of these statements are familiar: I don't feel enough (my former limiting self-talk); I feel too much; my feelings aren't powerful enough; my feelings are too powerful; I'm too sensitive and vulnerable; I'm too closed off and cold; I can't take criticism; I have good reason to be numb; I'm afraid I'm just not talented enough; I'm easily damaged and overwhelmed; I'm terribly shy; I have reason to be cynical; I'm not giving enough; I always give too much and then I get hurt…. The list could go on and on. Such emotional baggage, regardless of the story variation it perpetuates, is just that: a story—and one which can be transformed.

The Depths

When I followed my dream to live fully as a writer, a new dream revealed itself. I knew I was also called to guide others on the creative path. At first this twofold vision seemed paradoxical. On the one hand, I was learning as much as I could about creativity and personal development. My study intensified and my life evolved as a beautiful, albeit at times scary, adventure. I was committed to helping people live inspired, fulfilled, and happy lives. That meant teaching others effective techniques for replacing negative messages and emotions with positive, uplifting thoughts and feelings in harmony with their newly expanding visions. At the same time, I was committed even more whole-heartedly in my fiction to exploring the darkness—the minor keys—with characters whose journeys took us ever into the depths. This tension of opposites gave me life, but it also baffled me.

In my new situation, I was confronted with an age-old question: Why are some of us called to plumb the dark depths in our creativity anyway? Part of me wondered if I still desired to go into emotionally tough, gritty places in my fiction. The answer I received was "Yes." I held fast to Zen Roshi Joan Halifax's words on rites of initiation, as so often my characters have taken me such places. In myriad ways, they continue to reveal for me what Halifax describes as "those great zones of darkness that make the unclear, the contradictory, the polluted, and the changeable the ground of renewal." She describes such passages as "the occasions of fruitful darkness." For me, the whole process of receiving a story into the world is fruitful—that impulse to move through darkness into light, to harvest the gifts of those zones of becoming.

Through art, a seeker is able to gain insight, at times even an experience of healing, certainly of compassion, in exploring the shadowy regions of human experience. When I was a young teacher, I defended children who sought to read and write frightening or sad, intensely emotional stories. As a child I too had been drawn to tales of darkness, and I understood their cathartic and instructive power. For a long time I've subscribed to Bruno Bettelheim's view that the world of "unsanitized" fairy tales offers children a safe place to explore life's scarier situations. I believe it's the same for adults: many of us like our narratives in a minor key. With that said, I also believe in the power of a redemptive arc in fiction—not something contrived or imposed, but a natural coming about, an ascent after the journey downward and, often, inward. The hero's journey is deeply embedded in us; when children read, they instinctively look for a return home. I believe adults do, too—even, and perhaps especially, when that home is transformed.

Asked about the process of writing dark material, acclaimed Canadian author Margaret Atwood is said to have responded that it's all right to go to the underworld; just don't eat the food. Where would Aristotle have experienced pity and fear, and ultimately catharsis, had the theatrical tragedies of his day not existed? When creating from an authentic place of emotion, it's important to heed the call via whatever genre or form wants to come through. But we must be skillful divers. Know the limit and swim up to breathe and regain a sense of light and balance in your human experience. I love Julia Cameron's cautionary advice for artists to "keep the drama on the page." When I learned to do a better job of that, my writing became more courageous, more sustained, and more willing to take me deep into the shadows—and my life became much happier.

I also agree with Cameron that creators must find and trust their own "veins of gold." Obviously, that's not to say that art need be emotionally intense and serious to be beautiful, cathartic, and, on some level, redemptive. Simply discover what you're called to do, and do it. That means being open to receive. Whatever the genre or form of your work, whether you predominantly create in a minor or major key, or prefer the provocative cacophony of artistic discord—find the range of feeling beneath the work. As we all know, some of the greatest comedy has come through people intimately familiar with sadness. When feelings arise, they need to be seen, not stifled. That sacred seeing is part of cultivating awareness, and it doesn't mean we have to dwell in the sad and angry places. On the contrary. We can learn to recognize and shift negative emotion when it arises. But to *know* emotions, to recognize and fully feel, means we stay open, ever, to the possibility of experiencing a child's delight, and also to having empathy for the spectrum of human experience. When I studied singing, my teacher encouraged me to open my range as far as I could: "In order to go high you must go low." Such is the world of duality. In opening to the full potential of our creative experience, we make welcome the element of surprise that Frost writes about. The best sad stories often include belly laughs, too.

You can be a tragedy writer, an edgy photographer, an atavistic abstract painter, a postapocalyptic film director, a satirical poet, a brilliant stand-up comic—in short, the creator you were made to be—and still employ constructive personal development techniques in your life. I believe we come here to serve, and that in that essential act of connection we discover we are free. Art (indeed, all heart-centered creative enterprise) is a form of service, even when it feels like the creator only serves her or his own daimon. I borrow that term for an unseen force in the universe that compels us to fulfill our destiny from Swiss psychiatrist Carl Jung. In *Memories, Dreams, Reflections*, he writes, "A creative person has little power over his own life. He is not free. He is captive and driven by his daimon." This statement always gives me pause. On one level, I love that it reminds me to have compassion for myself and others like me, people compelled to live their passions and to sacrifice things others wouldn't for the opportunity to create in alignment with their character and calling. On another level, I embrace the paradox that choosing to live in the "grip" of one's daimon is actually freeing. When we listen to, and heed, a sacred voice from within, we're released from the cage. We're free to dive, free to fly, and sometimes simply free to float on the sun-dappled waters of life.

Such freedom can play tricks, causing us to see the creative work we love as a monumental challenge or, at the very least, a series of problems to solve. That was my experience of apprehension, going back into the depths of character work. But oh, how I loved it. And I always had! In his illuminating book on creativity, *Flow*, Mihaly Csikszentmihalyi discusses the necessity of rising to challenges for deep, personal satisfaction. When we work in the zone of mastery, tackling creative problems is *exactly* the route to happiness. Csikszentmihalyi writes that often we don't even recognize our deep happiness when engaged in the creative act of problem solving. So absorbed are we in the challenge that we seem to transcend emotion and a sense of time. In the zone, we discover ideas beyond our usual range of access. We learn to experience happiness in hindsight—and to make sacrifices in order to keep that experience in the forefront of our lives.

Happiness in the freedom to rise to challenges, to find new frontiers of knowing and creating, can bring us to tears—and sometimes to a place even deeper:

> Thanks to the human heart by which we live,
> Thanks to its tenderness, its joys and fears,
> To me the meanest flower that blows can give
> Thoughts that do often lie too deep for tears.

The poet William Wordsworth speaks those lines from "Intimations of Immortality" to me anew each time I read them. Engaging in vision-driven, heart-centered creativity is an experience "out of time." Suddenly it doesn't matter how many dives we make. Leonardo da Vinci spent seven years painting the *Mona Lisa*. When asked why he still practiced music each day at the age of ninety, legendary cellist

Pablo Casals replied, "Because I think I'm making progress."

Discernment

I studied Henrik Ibsen's plays as a young drama student. But I didn't come to fully appreciate them until I saw them performed onstage many years later. My favorite is *The Wild Duck*; its poignancy moves me deeply. Moreover, its connections to the potential pitfalls of the creative process are profound.

The story centers on two very different male characters. One is Hialmar Ekdal, a photographer of modest means living happily with his loving wife, Gina, and their fourteen-year-old daughter, Hedwig. The other is Gregers Werle, the brooding, idealistic son of a wealthy landowner, Hakon Werle. Gregers returns home after many years away, in order (as he sees it) to right the wrongs of the past. Galvanized by a sense of moral duty, he takes it upon himself to "relieve" Hialmar of his ignorance by revealing his wife Gina's long-ago affair with Gregers' father, Hakon. The results are devastating. Hialmar reacts rashly as, in his mind, all he'd once considered foundational is rocked: his loving marriage, even the paternity of his child. In sudden bitterness and rage, Hialmar rejects his wife's emotional appeals and distances himself from the family he has loved so dearly.

Early in the play, before Gregers' revelation, the audience learns that the young girl, Hedwig, and the man she cherishes as her father, Hialmar, have rescued a wild duck shot by Hakon Werle. The old man's shot had damaged the bird's wing, and the animal dove to the bottom of the lake to drown itself by clinging to the weeds. Werle's dog, however, retrieved it. Hedwig takes creative delight in an entire attic menagerie of found animals, and the duck she and Hialmar saved is her greatest source of pride. The bird comes to symbolize various things in the play. Initially, it marks the co-creative experience of a loving adult protector and child; it's an emblem of their life force and emotional bond.

The duck is also a creature which has clung to the murky depths, suggestive of a willful hiding. That's certainly the way Gregers Werle views Hialmar: as one in the dark who would do better to be "retrieved" into the light of what Gregers perceives as the truth—i.e., the facts. Here we see the crucial distinction between facts and truth go tragically unrecognized by the players. The facts are one thing, the emotional truth of Hialmar's situation quite another. Hialmar allows himself to be blinded by facts which have come to light and to ignore the deeper truth of his situation—that he has much to be grateful for and *in*: he belongs to a true family. Hialmar is a cherished part of a loving whole. In his temporary blindness, this character serves as a cautionary reminder that we all make choices as to how we perceive our experiences. We can react to facts, or we can choose to see the truth regardless of the present circumstances. This ability to discern the difference between facts and truth is one of the most important survival tools of any creative individual. It is a gift of maturity. Sadly, few young people are equipped to parse the light of truth from the murky and turbulent waters of adult dramas.

Eventually, in the attic, the winged bird comes to be regarded as an alien creature bound by limitation. Out of place, the duck is like the child, Hedwig, whose vision literally dims with disease and whose life force eventually shrinks in the midst of the emotional chaos around her. Hedwig overhears her parents arguing; Hialmar exclaims he'd like to wring the duck's neck. Gregers convinces Hedwig to sacrifice the wild duck for her father's happiness by asking her grandfather to shoot the animal. Instead, Hedwig shoots herself. Unable to see and feel beyond the pain of perceived rejection, abandonment, and the illusion of not belonging, she dies instantly by a bullet through the breastbone.

Nothing is more heartbreaking than a child's deep and profound anguish at feeling rejected. People underestimate how horrifyingly real and overwhelming a young person's emotions can be. Many of us have learned to cope with sharp emotions by dulling them through various survival methods. One is through giving up on our dreams. Another is through substance addiction—and of course the two are not mutually exclusive. We live in a society that rewards "getting through the day" with a drink. Make that two or three—at least in my case, when I was a young, then a not-so-young woman. When diagnosed with diabetes at the ripe old age of twenty-eight, the first question I asked my doctor was "Will I be able to drink?" In the landmark book *You Can Heal Your Life*, which I discovered several years later in a post-marital-breakup moment of apartment-laundry-room grace, Louise Hay links diabetes with "the sweetness gone out of life."

Certainly, I developed the disease when I believed that art had gone from my life. I felt like that winged bird. Yet I was relieved by the diagnosis, as I'd feared the onset of something worse. Diabetes was a disease I could manage, like I'd learned to manage my emotions by keeping them numb or buried. When they did surface, they came in tidal waves. But most of the time—nothing. A pleasant smile. A busy day. Wine. Sleep. Now, not a day goes by when I'm not grateful for having broken that pattern.

Art calls for emotional truth. The artist, who keeps the child inside alive by entering constantly into the state of play and creation, is vulnerable. It takes the tremendous courage and steadfast faith of an adult to persevere through rejection, to see beauty in the whole of creation, and to protect the inner child by, as psychologist Abraham Maslow put it, "being independent of the good opinions of others." I'm reminded of how many brilliant young artists don't survive. At such times, I am thankful for accessing a power greater than I, for the strength to persevere through the endurance tests of young adulthood—specifically, young womanhood—and to still be an artist. I'm relieved that I'm not a young woman anymore—so fraught with passion, so raw in seeing and expressing, so tortured by the illusion of not fitting or belonging, so unaccepting of my own authenticity.

I think of the luminary young photographer Francesca Woodman, who committed suicide at twenty-two after experiencing rejection and subsequent severe depression. From adolescence, she had developed her craft with mature and meticulous attention to detail. She'd explored the frontiers of composing the self-portrait, of seeing and depicting the female nude; she'd taken enormous risks in developing her own aesthetic. While at first glance, she may not have "belonged" in certain established circles of her time and place, she belonged in another timeless circle of challengers and visionaries. When I look at Woodman's compelling work, some of it turned down by the critics of her day, I remember to persevere and persist through everything—to know that what's inside each of us is greater than any present circumstance. How I wish I could see where her art would have taken her, had she lived. I think of the many young artists who have succumbed to the pressures of perceived failure—and of success: Amy Winehouse, Kurt Cobain, Jean-Michel Basquiat, Janis Joplin, Jimi Hendrix, Jim Morrison, and River Phoenix, to name but a few.

    I dedicate this chapter to all of you who, at any age, dare to risk bravely for the work you love, and to create from the heart.

    You belong.

On the beach, I sat with the body of the duck for a long time: my gift of the day. I decided to save its wings to remind me to dive deep—to not be afraid—and to return stronger. It took force to remove the wings with wire cutters. They were strong, beautiful wings, those hollow bones tougher than I'd thought.

    Don't be afraid of emotion as you craft and create. Let it come or not come—either way, it tells you a love story. Your whole life is a love story. Love the creative child within you unconditionally. Without unconditional love and acceptance from within, you are vulnerable in the worst way—a bird relying on a branch instead of on her own wings. Such reliance only upon externals is dangerous, potentially to the point of destruction. With love and acceptance from within, you are vulnerable in the best way, making a gift of your vulnerability, your feelings, and your deep connection in this world.

Claiming the Duck's Gift:
Freeing Your Emotions and Discernment

Exercise 1: Constructive Vulnerability in the Service of Your Dream

This exercise builds your courage muscles in a new way, by allowing you to get used to a feeling of healthy and constructive vulnerability as you tackle challenging aspects of creative work. No sooner had I typed a first draft of this exercise than I spoke with Peter, a dear writer friend of mine, who described the process of having to go back into a novel he'd finished eight months ago in order to write new scenes and explore a new character that had been undeveloped in his narrative. In our call, Peter described his fear of having to do the very thing I call "diving"—re-entering the work with a view to going deep, finding gifts, and creating authentically, anew. He was acting on a publisher's request, and the stakes were high. This situation occurs often in the creative process; just when we think we're finished something, that we can stand and admire it, we're called back inside to make changes. Our entire range of creative faculties must be readily available to us, including our emotions and a willingness to feel vulnerable yet, at the same time, to persist. In fact, feeling vulnerable is often the very signpost that tells us we're on the right path.

Brené Brown has contributed much to the field of understanding and championing our human willingness to be vulnerable. She makes and supports the argument that the willingness to be vulnerable is required for growth and connection. If you aren't already familiar with her work, I recommend you explore it. Brown writes, "Vulnerability is the birthplace of innovation, creativity, and change." She describes spending years trying to "outrun or outsmart vulnerability by making things certain and definite, black and white, good and bad." Brown goes on to state, "My inability to lean into the discomfort of vulnerability limited the fullness of those important experiences that are wrought with uncertainty: love, belonging, trust, joy, and creativity, to name a few." The exercise that follows is meant to help you build the constructive capacity to be vulnerable in the service of a meaningful and fulfilling creative dream.

In your journal, make a pact with yourself that during and after the entire following activity you are safe, even when you don't feel that way. Call upon the adult in you to establish a protected space for your creative inner child to communicate freely and honestly. This may mean ensuring that you're home alone, or you have access to a room with a closed door. Symbolize the safety in this space by lighting a candle—a reminder that even in the darkest place there is light. This work is for your eyes only and the experience is transitory. Any time we dive, the point is not to stay down but to resurface with the gifts of the journey. This exercise is not about wallowing, even if it feels that way for a little while; it's about courageously seeing, feeling, and listening—and ultimately taking positive action.

Brainstorm a list of actions you could take, in the service of your dream, which up until now have triggered feelings of fear and vulnerability. Identify where you have been stuck. Below is a list of questions to help you think of examples. It wasn't difficult for me to make this list, because I am familiar with all of the situations on it. I am continually cycling through my own areas of resistance. Remember, no one has to see your list but you. The more aware you become of your challenges, and the more willing you become to work through such transitory blocks, the more assured of success you are. If you're tempted to skip this activity, lean into it all the more.

- Are you afraid of beginning, investing in, writing, painting, studying for, researching, rehearsing, composing, or in any other way creating a part—or all—of a current project? If so, what holds you back? Moreover, what is your choice to hold back costing you?—and are you willing to continue paying that price? If the answer to that last question is no, then what would it take for you to get past the perceived obstacle?
- Is there a picture you're compelled to paint, or a story you're compelled to write, that scares you? If so, why? Can you bless

the project idea and let it go? If that doesn't feel right, what steps can you take steps to let the work get through?
- Are you afraid to revise an aspect of your current creative project because you worry about ruining it? If so, what is it costing you *not* to revise it?
- Are you afraid of finishing a creative project? If so, why? What is it costing you to leave the work unfinished? What would it take to move through this perceived obstacle and bring your work to completion?
- Are you hesitant to share a piece of work for constructive feedback? If so, why? Be very specific about your fears in this regard. What is it costing you not to share the work? What steps could you take to face your fear?
- Is there a project you currently hold onto—perhaps one which has been your teacher—which you now suspect you are meant to release? Ask yourself if the benefits of holding on outweigh the costs. If they do, then seek to understand why, and to intuit the next steps for moving forward to see the project realized. If not, identify the steps you can take in releasing the work, affirming, "This, or something greater still." Expect something greater! Know that when you release a project, your creative power remains undiminished.
- Is there a person connected with your creative work with whom you feel reluctant to communicate? If so, identify what in you is causing the reluctance. Avoid blaming; take ownership of your feelings. Have you ever rehearsed a different and more positive dynamic with the person in question? If not, you may wish to try that: What would your ideal conversation with that person be? Imagine it fully, with your emotions and five senses. Plant the seeds of positive energy there. Keep up this effort for at least twenty-one days in order to change the relationship dynamic inwardly before expecting different results in the outer, experiential world. If you decide that the relationship isn't worth working on, then what steps could you take with integrity and

courage in order to release it and move forward?
- Is there an area of self-promotion you've been avoiding? Can you identify an aspect of social media which, if it were to be well developed, would help you to advance your creative work? What, if anything, holds you back? At what cost? What small steps could you take today, and the rest of this week, to move forward? What could you do to make change happen sooner rather than later?
- Is your perfectionism holding you back in any area of your creative work? I have found my own to be an obstacle over the years—one I'm constantly staring down. What harm comes from being overly cautious? Can you see ways that too much caution can be as potentially harmful as not being cautious at all?

Spend a while on the task of questioning and responding, really exploring stories from your experience. You are the hero of all of them, the star of your own life. What dramas have you been seemingly forced to endure? What perceived obstacles have you created along the way?

Then ask yourself what steps you can take right now to overcome those obstacles and move forward in the service of your creative dream. Seek for clarity and inner guidance in this area. When you have identified some steps, begin taking them—today. Create a schedule and commit to following through. Remember Emerson's words: "Every wall is a door." Move forward in the spirit of expansion and creative growth.

This assignment is intimate: it's between you and you. Resist the temptation to drink alcohol, sip caffeine, or partake of any other mood-altering substance while you do it. Come to the page as emotionally present as you can be, and make a pact to take care of yourself through whatever reveals itself. You are safe. Decide on a time limit—thirty minutes or an hour—and set an alarm to reassure yourself you will stick to it. As you respond and take action based on your responses, experiment with feeling vulnerable. So much of life is a glorious experiment when we let it be just that.

After you've finished this exercise, give yourself a big win! Close with a powerful gratitude activity in order to raise and reset your emotional vibration. An attitude of gratitude is the best starting point for all creativity. Write ten things you're grateful for and really savor them. Take your gifts and your gratitude on a long walk.

Exercise 2: Welcoming Joy

The benefits of laughter are many. Regardless of the nature of your creative work, laughing each day is beneficial not only to your creativity, but to your health. I knew a woman who, when going through a challenging time in her personal life, committed to watching funny movies in the evenings. Laughter became her number-one therapy, and she pulled through beautifully. If you don't have time to watch an entire film in the evening, search for scenes you've loved in the past and enjoy them on the Internet. Give yourself this pleasure on a break at work with headphones. Laughter is contagious—pass it on!

You can also induce laughter simply by laughing. You may wish to do this exercise when you're alone—or not: just laugh. Really belly-laugh (yes, *make* it happen instead of waiting for that elusive blue bird), and find out what happens to your body and mental attitude. Mary Morrissey taught me this technique, and I confess I still need to remind myself to practice it daily; when I do, I always enjoy it. Creativity loves joy. My favorite Abraham Lincoln quote is this one: "Most folks are as happy as they make their minds up to be." Make up your mind to laugh, today and every day.

What brings you joy? Make a list of activities you love. Pick at least three things and do them before the week's out.

Exercise 3: Soundtracking

I've used this technique for many years because I know that regardless of the mood I'm in, I can rely on music to open me emotionally in my creative work—even on those rare days when I don't feel like writing. On my walks, I know I can use music to enter the mood required for whatever task awaits. I often listen to carefully selected instrumental pieces when I write. In fact, music in my ears is a helpful way of putting a protective sound bubble around my creative process when I write in cafés. I enjoy the bustle of public places, yet when I'm creating, I need my emotional space, and music gives it to me.

I invite you to use music consciously and purposefully to evoke emotion in your creative process. Here are some examples of how music can be used constructively. Choose any of the suggestions from this list and make them your own—and of course, find more.

- Select music you love, a sound that really evokes strong passion in you, and listen while you paint, move, make notes, and draft.
- Find mood music for easy access to the emotion required for a certain scene you're writing, assemblage you're constructing, vision you're laying out, etc.
- In the process of inviting and receiving information about a character, make ideas welcome by choosing soundtrack music for your process. Some of my characters have their own theme songs, which elicit an immediate emotional connection within me each time I return to work.
- Find uplifting, inspirational music for your visioning work. When you mentally picture a beautiful aspect of your dream unfolding, underscore it with music that contributes to a sense of joy in beholding your dream come true.
- Listen to uplifting music in the car while you drive. While being fully present to traffic, experience the feeling of your dream come true. This is a victory drive! Each time you're stopped at a

light, feel gratitude that your creative vision has been realized. (This exercise can transform the way you see red lights!)

Key Ideas

- Be aware of old, limiting self-talk around your emotions and creativity. Whatever old stories have held you back can be transformed. Recognize when you're caught in a story and replace that story with a new one.
- Art is made through full-spectrum feeling in both the artist and the co-creative receiver. Our range of emotion is the life force of our experience of art.
- The darkness can be fruitful when we learn to recognize its gifts, which include vulnerability, discernment and resilience.
- We must not hesitate to dive in the service of creativity, but must learn to contain our dives.
- The necessity of rising to creative challenges brings happiness—though oftentimes, only in hindsight.
- For any of us, the solution to painful feelings must not be to dull emotions, or manage them through artificial means. Conscious creativity calls for full awareness and emotional truth.
- It takes mature courage and faith to persevere through rejections, to see beauty in the whole of creation and to protect the inner child, who is a natural visionary.
- Persevere and persist through any and all perceived obstacles to creative fulfillment; know that what's inside you is greater than your present circumstances. You have access to a source of strength and intelligence far greater than you know.
- Joy is a great re-balancer. Make it welcome each day. Laugh!
- Love yourself unconditionally, and know that you are loved.

Chapter 6
The Swan:
Freeing Recognition

Endurance is a gift, not a trial.
—Joan Halifax

Creating Your Self and Your World

You have the power to create the story of your experience. This is an essential understanding, and one I encourage you to return to habitually as you navigate the beautiful journey of your life. This ability to hold the thought you choose in the face of present circumstances is an awesome gift. You can shift from reacting to life's facts to responding thoughtfully and skilfully from your creative center. With awareness and practice, any of us can learn to hold to our truth, regardless of the facts. This book is about learning to see the beauty in all experience, even in the face of apparent challenges and setbacks. It's about recognizing and honoring a creative calling, and staying faithful to it. Those are not the words of a Pollyanna. They are not mere "cheer up, be positive, things will turn out fine" words, but a serious and sober directive. The advice to respond rather than react to life's challenges may at first seem simplistic; indeed, the process *is* simple. But it is not easy.

Making the shift from programmed reacting to thoughtful, creative responding requires commitment, open-mindedness, and a willingness to experiment. Repetition is the key to mastering any skill. When employed repeatedly, the process of responding rather than reacting makes a breakthrough not only possible, but welcome. We cannot engineer breakthroughs in our lives, but we can make them welcome. Trust in possibilities that you still can't see from your present vantage point by learning to see all the good in your present situation. Seeing with new eyes is nothing short of grace.

The swan is a traditional symbol of grace. It is also, of course, the creature whose self-recognition we celebrate in Hans Christian Andersen's classic children's story "The Ugly Duckling." Ted Andrews identifies the swan as the totem of the child, the poet, the mystic and the dreamer: "It can show how to see the inner beauty within yourself or in others, regardless of outer appearances." I love the invitation in the words "how to see." Here, the creative possibilities are expansive; we are encouraged to read beneath the surface of appearance, into the depths of meaning that only we can make. Stephen Farmer picks up on this message in his book *Power Animals* when he encourages us to witness not only our own inner beauty but the beauty which surrounds us. "You're no ugly duckling. Neither is your world, even with all its dark and shadowy elements," writes Farmer. "It's always for you to choose to notice the magical dance of shadow and light in all its mystery and allure, without fear of judgment." Whom do you see when you look in the mirror? How do you feel about the face staring back at you? Where are you in your magnificent story?

If present circumstances feel like a trial, can you see them as a gift? When you look at yourself in the present moment, all facts considered, do you recognize the beauty? So many people don't, because we're seldom taught this way of creative, expansive thinking. In choosing to evolve, we must learn to overcome more than one level of conditioning. The oldest part of the brain, the stem, contains the reactive "fight or flight" mechanism designed to ensure our survival in the wild. When an experience appears bad or threatening, our first reaction is to be aggressive—to lash out in anger and destructive thoughts, or to flee—to abandon the situation, to avoid or escape entirely. Either way, we lose a sense of centeredness and confidence. It takes consistent effort over time to learn to re-route mental processing from the reactive amygdala in the brain stem to the pre-frontal cortex. The swan reminds us of our capacity to sustain clear-sightedness and calm. This powerful bird has often been associated with dignity and magic. Farmer encourages us to ask symbolically for the swan's help when we need "a strong dose of poise and confidence."

The ability to look in the mirror and recognize that your power is greater than your present circumstance is vital to your creativity. In his book of essays on writing, *A Way of Being Free,* Nigerian poet and novelist Ben Okri provides these words of reassurance:

> There is no need to panic. The intelligence that shaped the universe shaped you. There is an inner part of us, for ever obscured, for ever mysterious, which is most alive during the process of composition.... It drinks from deep waters. It has the stillness and the dance and the radiance of the firmament.... Creativity makes us part of it all. There is no genuine creative or human problem that cannot be solved if you are serene enough, humble enough, and if you have learnt the gentle arts of concentration, visualization, and meditation. For me, tranquility is the sign of the invincible presence of grace.

I reflect on the word "composition" and think of the dignity inherent in gifting the world with one's story. I'm not talking about a book, film, or painting, but of *your story*—the way you choose to read and write your life. When you can read your story as beautiful, regardless of the specific facts of the moment, you become, as Andrews says, "a magnet to others." The very act of choosing tranquility, of reflecting and composing, allows your composure to shine as a light for others.

That can sound like a tall order, however, when you feel like your world is falling apart.

Dangers, Toils, and Snares

When I look back on the toughest moments of my life, I recognize my old pattern of escaping pain rather than trusting it to teach me. Trusting meant accepting it in the first place, which seemed like an injustice because I'd had my share. I was fed up with pain. It seemed to meet me around every corner. There were times when, as a young woman, aspects of my life felt like a cruel joke. My dream of being an artist had seemed real—I had believed I could bet on it utterly (or had told myself I believed), and the blow and shock of rejection in my chosen field felt insurmountable. I literally made myself sick over it.

For years I gave myself over to the study of literature, wanting to immerse myself in that world forever, only to feel like a victim of necessity, forced to return to the world of gainful employment—to working with children, whose lives truly were blessings and wonders, although sadly I was forgetful of that truth sometimes. Mine was a hard way to enter teaching. Initially, the burden of my responsibilities seemed to far outweigh my blessings, and I compounded that burden by masking it—making everything seem "all right." My marriage was crumbling. Relationships were transporting me quickly to places where I could hide, if only for a moment. Every foundation I created seemed to fall apart. I saw heartbreak as a brutal and exacting external force, constantly waiting for me in the wings like the monsters of my childhood nightmares.

It took me years to come to terms with my own complicity in the series of calamities that characterized my life. It was a painful pattern that I had to not only recognize but comprehend and address in order to change. In my mid-thirties, after going through a particularly tough breakup—the short-lived relationship had sown the seeds of its own destruction from the start—I finally recognized my standard operating procedure of self-punishment. This time, instead of wallowing in anguish and leaping to another romantic distraction that couldn't last, I chose to pause and look at my life squarely. "There is no genuine creative or human problem that cannot be solved if you are serene enough, humble enough…." For the first time, I realized the profoundly healing power of humility.

What scares us often frees us; humility was the scariest place I'd been.

Part of me hated relinquishing control. All my life, I'd believed that being humble meant giving up my self-esteem and removing the armour I'd created out of a strong urge to survive. That armour was made up of self-identifiers such as "safe," "talented," "successful," "highly functional," "smart," "high achieving," "noteworthy," and "untouchable." What it shielded was an acutely sensitive child, one who, like so many of us, still carried emotional wounds in her unhealed adult body. For much of my life I'd feared that if I trusted in humility, all the critics and doubters would be right about me: I'd be doomed to live out my life as a meek failure who was never good enough to fulfill her dream, always coming just short. Deep down, I was my own biggest critic and doubter; I'd convinced myself I wasn't going to be fulfilled—that I somehow didn't deserve it, or simply couldn't "pull it off."

I felt wretched that my choices had caused pain. Once again, synchronicity plucked me from the doldrums. I shared my experience with a friend, who recommended a great therapist. For once I was too vulnerable and heartbroken to flash the armour. I made an appointment the same day.

One of the breakthroughs that occurred when I recognized the gifts in my perceived hardship, including the gift of opening my eyes to my own mistaken beliefs and addictive tendencies, was letting go of alcohol. Perhaps because my heartbreak over the end of my relationship was so acute, so profound, giving up the drink(s)-a-day habit came surprisingly easily. Sipping wine in the evenings had always been something I'd managed, like so much else; I knew how to limit, though honestly I was beginning to push the boundary. Certainly, I'd always been highly functional in my work. Others close to me insisted I didn't have a problem, but I knew differently. A glass of wine sapped my energy, limited my creativity, and made it easy to default to my old patterns. I'm not suggesting this is true for everyone, or passing judgment on social drinking. I've met many people who have no difficulty taking a drink or leaving it. I just knew that I personally needed help to make a significant shift in behavior—because I found it hard to stop at one.

I made the decision to enter a twelve-step program, which begins with an admission of powerlessness over alcohol. For the first time, accepting powerlessness felt like the only option for me if I wanted to effect real change. I finally looked in the mirror and read hope in the lines on my face. I could *decide* on a better journey. Revisiting an unvarnished version of my past, I recognized what I needed in order to invite experience and a power higher than me to be my teacher. It was a tough moment because it hurt, and I wouldn't wish that pain on anyone. Yet my melancholy was also tinged with a sense of relief and liberation—which eventually turned to joy. It was a critical juncture so essential to my development that I only have gratitude for it now, looking back, when I can see the dots connected so clearly in hindsight.

In retrospect, each "failure" was an opportunity I missed, with more perceived failures patiently waiting to teach me. Now that I have come to understand and change a pattern of attracting painful experiences I once labelled as failures—to see such experiences as feedback—I celebrate that I can also learn from happiness. I strive to do so every day.

Learning to See into the Life of Things

In my healing and growth process I came to recognize the incredible beauty of the connections in my life. My teaching work, which at times had felt like servitude, became meaningful, heartfelt service. I gave myself to teaching in ways that it had been calling me to for years. I also committed to being an emotionally available, stable, dependable, nurturing mother for my beloved daughter. And while I sometimes fell short of my goal, I pray, just as I'm sure my own loving mother and father do, that today my adult child recognizes

I did my best with what I knew and what I had at the time. I think all us who are reflective, honest parents have no greater prayer than for our love to be stronger than our weaknesses, our unwitting negligence, our oldest sad stories and our fears. In humility we pray, knowing that from an imperfect nest of our own making, and by a power greater than we are, a beautiful being emerges and takes flight.

I could never have made those breakthroughs without humility and a belief that I was living on purpose. During this period of my life, my journal became a safe haven in which to process and reflect on transformation. In taking a stand for a better life, I also voted for calm, for laughter, and for the creative expression in me—which didn't cower, as I'd feared it might, but which came forth more strongly and clearly than ever. Suddenly, with the wine routine gone, I had the creative energy, time, and vision to write fiction. I committed to the process wholeheartedly, even though I knew it might take me years to bring the first story and its sequels into form while I taught full-time. I knew I'd need to be patient and live in alignment with my values in order to lovingly give over much of my time each year to parenting and teaching. I couldn't see beyond the headlights on that particular stretch of road, but I took the risk to trust my creativity. My journal accompanied me everywhere I went, an emblem of my faith, even though for many weeks of the year I could only write my morning pages and evening reflections. I learned to recognize my life as a beautiful unfolding.

In an essay entitled "Spiritual Laws," Emerson writes, "We discover that our life is embosomed in beauty." Things, he tells us, "have a grace in the past." I have found this to be true—although we do not always recognize grace when we see it. I urge you to train your eyes to see the grace in your own life, even if it doesn't always look like you anticipated it would.

While writing this section of *Birdlight*, I took a break and traveled to New England with my husband, Hugh—my soul mate, who appeared in my life at exactly the right time, when we both were ready. In Boston, I saw many a swan: swan boats, Audubon swans, and swan ornaments. All were reminders to me to see with new eyes. When I returned home to Toronto, I watched majestic swans glide and splash on Grenadier Pond, and I still carry a white feather to remind me of grace in this world. For me, sometimes grace comes in the gratitude I feel in being in love with my soul mate, laughing and sharing stories of our adventures over dinner. Sometimes grace comes in enjoying the sunshine in late April even if the temperature is still below freezing. Sometimes grace comes when I return to school and feel the warmth, vitality, and inspiration amongst dear students and colleagues. Grace is delighting in new possibilities as they present themselves—like this book that I didn't see coming, and the discovery of a calling not only to write, but to serve others in their creative dreams and pursuits.

There is also grace in the experience of working with young people again—this time in a new way. Several months after starting this book and beginning to build my coaching practice, I found myself delighting in a beautiful transition phase, helping students one on one as both a tutor and a coach. Every young person in my life has been, and continues to be, a gift. I've learned from two great teachers, Mary Morrissey and Peggy McColl, that my vocation doesn't have to be an "either/or"; it can be a "both/and." I can be a focused, serious artist and contributor in more than one capacity. My sense of connection with community and service ushered in that expansive recognition.

Recognition: "The Ugly Duckling"

I appreciate Hans Christian Andersen's story "The Ugly Duckling" now even more than I did as a child. This timeless fable imparts much about universal patterns in the human journey. The story begins with ducklings hatching. Their mother assures them that the world is larger than they think, yet she won't dare to venture to the edge of the garden. To her credit, and despite her impatience for the last egg to hatch, she doesn't act on the advice of the neighbor who urges her to abandon the "slow" egg, adding it must belong to a turkey. When the egg finally hatches, the mother duck initially accepts her strange young offspring as soon as she sees that he can swim. In accepting him as her own, she also makes sure to instill in him her paradigm of a dangerous world: one must stay close to home; one must beware of the cat; and the way of the world is fighting.

When her youngest "duckling" is bullied for his strange appearance, the mother defends him. When the bullying becomes physical abuse, she eventually wishes he'd never been born.

The ugly duckling's first home is populated by other ducks that peck and jeer at him, a cat that wants to eat him, chickens that beat him, a poultry girl who kicks him, and a turkey-cock that behaves like a petty emperor. Hardship drives the ugly duckling from his first home into a much larger world—yet while his world becomes larger, his worldview doesn't change. He expects a threatening, capricious landscape, and that's exactly what he gets. The wild ducks he meets take little interest in him. The geese that befriend him are shot dead. When his new environment is racked with a violent storm, the ugly duckling seeks shelter in an old woman's house, only to find himself in the presence of more petty rulers: a tomcat that fancies himself master and a mistress hen that denies the newcomer free speech and rights, instructing him to learn to purr and lay eggs and be grateful for his "good fortune." Thus, the alien young creature continues to attract hardship. The feeling of not fitting in eventually drives him into the big world again. Things begin to shift for him when, for the first time, he sees a bevy of swans. Too shy to come forward, yet thrilled by an intuitive sense of connection, he stays back while the swans fly off, and the ugly duckling almost perishes in the harsh winter that follows.

In a long-awaited spring, the ugly duckling discovers the swans again, and he resolves to be with the "royal birds" even if it means that he must die—for he is almost certain the swans will kill him. The humble seeker's willingness to take a major risk is crucial. For in moving toward his dream—that of union with the swans—and in seeing them welcome him, he finally looks at his own reflection in the water. In the tale's famous climax, he recognizes his identity as "no longer a dark, grey bird, ugly and disagreeable to look at, but a graceful and beautiful swan." Having seen his connection with something great of which he is a part and for which he's yearned, he gains a sense of new clarity. Moreover, when the swan recognizes his own power, grace, and connection, he changes his view of the past. He realizes that he not only is now, but always has been, the creature of his dreams. This recognition enables him "to enjoy so much better all the pleasure and happiness around him." When his view of himself changes, his world does, too. The other creatures see him differently, and the children love him.

The ugly duckling's story of endurance and discovery brings to mind a passage from Robert Collier's classic book *The Secret of the Ages*. Your difficulties, Collier says, are "an exercise of your mind. You are stronger for having overcome them." He goes on to assert that these "'stunts' are given you in order that you may the better learn how to use your mind, to draw upon Universal Supply." He advises, "Like Jacob wrestling the angel, don't let them go until they have blessed you—until, in other words, you have learned something from having encountered them." True self-recognition reveals our connection to something much greater than the self: our access to what Collier calls the Universal Mind and a deep knowing that we have the power not only to endure challenges, but to create constructively from them, and beyond them, in order to make our greatest dreams realities. Collier calls this recognition the "ark" of understanding: that each of us has access to universal, and enormously constructive, power.

For me, reflecting on the writings of Andersen and Collier elicits thoughts of several iconic historical figures who each reached a crucial point of recognition that allowed the old self to die into the new. The first one I think of is Nelson Mandela, who reached a critical point of recognition during his twenty-seven-year imprisonment on Robben Island. Mandela realized that if he was going to make a further difference in the world, to serve on a greater level, he would need to let the man who'd entered the jail—the angry young version of himself—die. By his own account, he left that prison a different person. During my elementary-school teaching days, I was very fortunate to see Mandela and hear him speak in Toronto in the company of children who revered him. Like the swan, he represented the grace of fulfilled potential: the ability to access a power far greater than his own and to harness that power for the common good. The children sensed it, and they celebrated it. They were captivated. Mandela was loving and respectful, and also deeply humble, gentle, and wise.

I also think of Mohandas Gandhi, who, by taking decisive and creative control of his life, evolved into Mahatma. He reached a point of recognition when, to fulfill a mission he was only then discovering, he understood that he needed to let the proud, British-educated Indian lawyer in a Savile Row suit die into a man whose dignity, values, and far-reaching impact necessitated a new way of being. I'm grateful to director Richard Attenborough for bringing that story to life so profoundly in the 1982 film *Gandhi*. I still remember seeing it as a teenager and being moved. Years later, I picked up Gandhi's translation of the *Bhagavad Gita* and read it; only now, however, can I say I'm prepared to *study* it. Attenborough's film created a path in me. I recently discovered that it took the director eighteen years to see that project realized; the story of its making is a testament to the artist's persistence in finding the right creative conditions and the necessary extraordinary team. Those conditions, along with Attenborough's burning desire, his faith and his patience, were essential to moving the project forward.

The theme of persistence makes me think of yet another icon of persistence and grace: Helen Keller—blind, deaf, and unable to speak—who permitted her sense of separation from the world to fall away in exchange for a sense of mission and connection. Her message for the world is her legacy: "Alone we can do so little, together we can do so much."

Of course, countless lesser known but equally powerful examples of self-recognition and transformation are around us every day. Such recognition can come at any age, but not surprisingly it most commonly occurs when we're older. In her inspirational work *Defying Gravity: A Celebration of Late-Blooming Women*, author Prill Boyle recounts case studies of contemporary women who made dramatic shifts in their careers at midlife. I applaud Boyle for overcoming her own challenges in bringing the book to light. Rejected by fourteen publishers, Boyle persevered and ultimately saw her creative dream realized at age fifty. I recommend *Defying Gravity* to anyone looking for role models of tenacity, vision, and courage. In each of the twelve stories, a woman's former world view of limitation, hurt, and anger had to die into the recognition of her creative power. Examples include a woman who entered medical school at forty-six and went on to practice in her fifties with a high degree of empathy and compassion, qualities which she refused to have "conditioned out" of her. She attributed her emotional resilience to her stage of life, convinced she had more to offer her patients after starting "late" than she would have had earlier. Another story features an African-American former teen mom who overcame severe poverty and abuse and entered college at twenty-nine. By age forty-nine, having worked steadily and raised her children as a single parent, she'd also earned her Ph.D. and been hired for a senior position at her college.

My favorite of Boyle's case studies concerns Jean Karotkin. After surviving breast cancer at thirty-eight, she decided to leave an unfulfilling marriage and become a professional photographer—even though she had no previous training or experience. Twelve years later, her work was featured in *Oprah* and *Rosie* magazines. Her book of photographs of breast cancer survivors, *Body & Soul*, was published to critical acclaim, its "influential portraits of women" revealing their ageless beauty and authenticity. In her interview with Boyle, Karotkin says, "I always tell people that my life began when I was diagnosed with breast cancer. In retrospect, though, I can see that everything that has happened to me has been for a purpose." She learned to use adversity constructively, transforming the struggles of her past into stories of grace in action.

In every story of self-recognition and transformation, a sense of connection to community and access to a power greater than one's own is crucial. Certainly if you are an artist determined to harness creativity in the service of a life-affirming dream, connections with others whose desires align with your constructive, creative vision are paramount.

Birds of a Feather

One of the greatest gifts I received years ago was recognizing that a higher power can speak to us not only through intuition but through others. It's absolutely vital to a person's creative growth process to find the right community to engage with. Be open to the guidance that comes, either directly or indirectly, from interacting with positive, experienced, skilled, and creative individuals. Remind yourself of how, in fulfilling your purpose, you too serve your community. No great artist creates alone.

I advise you to build your creative support crew by engaging with various success-oriented team players who fulfill different roles. Prepare to be a giver first—and give for the sake of giving. Only then do you create the conditions for receiving. That's how the karmic law of receiving works: the power is in the give. That includes giving of your talents and energy, but it also applies to investing in your dream by paying—willingly—for the help of people who've successfully done what you would love to do yourself. Money is simply energy. Bless each check you write as an affirmation of your dream becoming reality.

The first level of support—the bedrock—is mentorship. This was the crucial foundation missing for me when I was young. Without the support of a highly skilled creative mentor, I lacked the constructive thinking required to get me through the challenges inevitable in any artistic pursuit. I now have no doubt I had the right stuff to be the performer I'd dreamed of being; I had passion and fine ability. What I needed was a clearer vision and more training, as well as the nuanced prompting, understanding, guidance, and encouragement of a great coach. Self-help books are excellent, but they aren't the same as human contact. Beyond the realm of athletics, coaching wasn't common or widely known in the 1980s when I was, unwittingly, desperate for it. Fortunately, the situation has changed dramatically, and today coaching is an increasingly popular and far-reaching field.

In my transformation from a full-time schoolteacher to a full-time writer, and eventually to an author, coach, and speaker, the first thing I did was say yes to finding mentors. Acting on intuition, I responded to an e-mail message that appeared in my inbox one day. I paid more for a coaching program than I was comfortable paying; all my baggage around money came up. Yet I paid it anyway, because at that point my courage and desire had finally surpassed my fear. Engaging with a mentor, and later with other coaches, was a vote for building and sustaining the creative life of my dreams. The advice of preeminent coach Bob Proctor for anyone striving to make a dream come true is to find someone who's done what you want to do and then do what that person does.

I found Mary Morrissey, who taught me brave thinking.

While writing the first draft of this book, I was fortunate to go to Concord, Massachusetts, for a retreat with Mary. While we sat together at a small dinner gathering and I shared the story of the latest publishers' rejection letters I'd received for my novel while also talking of my newfound strength, Mary looked at me, eyes sparkling, and said, "Those publishers' rejection letters—they constitute your worthy opponent. You see, it's a perfect system." And then I really did see. The rejections were upping my game. In that moment, I was able to borrow on the power of her believing in my novel's success, and to keep moving forward.

After that conversation I resolved that not only would I *not* give up on the book (I'd distribute it to smaller presses and self-publish if I had to) but that I would allow myself to be open to making further revisions—something which had previously been unthinkable. Sure enough, while walking the road from Thoreau Rock to the Colonial Inn in Concord, I received an intuitive message—a "spiritual download" as I like to call it—and I knew immediately what small but significant changes I should make in the novel. I believe that unseen forces guide us in our heartfelt work, and that all of us have the ability to tune in.

While you make a point of being still each day and listening to an inner voice of wisdom, I invite you to take inventory. What strengths, knowledge, and skills do you already have, and which ones are missing from your toolkit? Be honest and, again, look fearlessly and with humility. Here is an opportunity to seek out teachers of your specific craft. I love Rosanne Cash's advice to songwriters to get their skills strong enough so that they can "catch" songs from the ether when they come. The same applies to artists of any creative path or medium—to anyone starting a new venture. We need teachers and other professionals to help guide us in our work so that our skills are up to the task. We need to be humble and receive the help. We almost invariably need a team, even if we are solo artists. Identify who you need on your team. Make a move in the direction of your vision by putting positive, successful people around you. Remember that success is a state of mind. Study with teachers whose gifts bring you life: a growing sense of confidence, expansiveness, and ability. If your response to a certain teacher is consistently contractive, to the point where you feel routinely disempowered, change teachers. You're not out for false compliments, but you *are* out to develop your confidence and vision along with your skill set. Intimidation is not conducive to growth. Find relationships that facilitate and nurture your growth. You can be humble in the presence of a great teacher and still build your confidence and skills.

I feel immensely fortunate to have cultivated relationships with many people who've helped me grow. In addition to intentionally inviting the right mentors and teachers into my experience, I've also discovered another level of guidance: the mastermind group. This is a group of two or more open-minded and goal-oriented creators committed to blessing and prospering one another on their respective chosen paths. The power of gathering with small groups to assist one another has led me to many new and important insights, business ideas, and immensely helpful connections. It can do the same for you.

In your journal, list the people in your life with whom you're actively engaged to prosper on your creative path. (Include only individuals you personally know and interact with.) Create categories: coaches and mentors, teachers in our chosen field, an accountability partner (for brief and positive weekly goal-setting), mastermind group members, and other business professionals (add any categories specific to your endeavor as needed). As of today, who is on your team? Who is missing? Schedule time one day this week to find and add at least one person to your list. Use your intuition. Invest in yourself and your community.

I believe in the angels among us; in the supportive communities we create as mastermind partners and as friends; and in the unseen forces whispering to us even when conditions look unfavorable—indeed, *especially* then, since the only difference between favorable and unfavorable situations may be our degree of perception and recognition. Others help us to see things positively. There is grace in communities. Marianne Williamson writes, "As we let our own light shine, we unconsciously give other people permission to do the same. As we are liberated from our fear, our presence automatically liberates others." Let your light shine, and you will see that no challenge is insurmountable.

Claiming the Swan's Gift:
Recognition through Forgiveness and Revision

As a writer and a student of life, I've come to accept that, at best, words only point to things. Nonetheless, words have real influence on our experience. We create with our words and thoughts, knowing that on some level, mystery is an ever-present partner. This is a book on creativity, not mysticism. Yet I suggest that when you treat your creative calling as spiritual, regardless of your predominant belief system, your calling and character point you to something you would do well to honor: your story. Whether you are a budding artist or one long established in a creative pursuit, I encourage you to learn to see your story in ways that enable you ever to grow. Here are two exercises that will help if you choose to practice them.

Exercise 1: Seeing with New Eyes

A statement I keep posted in large letters above my desk comes from James Allen's *As a Man Thinketh*: "Circumstance does not make the man; it reveals him to himself." We have the creative power to determine what's revealed. The beloved Buddhist teacher Thich Nhat Hanh writes that every human being contains the "seeds" of all the attributes we're capable of embodying in this earthly world—not only the myriad of life-affirming seeds, but also seeds of indifference, of anger in all its variations, of bitterness, envy, greed, and resentment, and even of hatred. Each of us contains the full spectrum of potential. Hanh urges us to choose which seeds we cultivate—to water only those we wish to see grow, letting the others wither. People who choose to see themselves primarily as victims attract and generate experience from a different frequency than those who perceive themselves primarily as empowered, life-affirming, and confident creative contributors. The following exercise is designed to remind you to honor your calling and character as you continue to create your world.

This activity calls for you to revisit the writing you did at the end of Chapter 1 ("The Owl"), when you listed perceived obstacles and saw the gifts they offered. Perhaps more stories of past challenges came up in your writing following other chapters. As always, the purpose is not to dwell in negative places, but to identify stories that have, up until now, persisted in draining you and blocking your creative confidence and growth. Take time to review, recall, and tap into your intuition as you list any obvious (and discover any not-so-obvious) remaining baggage.

Remember that the law of receiving requires you first to give. This may feel completely counterintuitive, yet it is a powerful law. If, up until now, old stories from the past have continued to weigh you down, I suggest you become very clear about what it is you'd love to gain from the circumstances of your life. For me, one word comes to mind: freedom. Imagine cultivating a real sense of being unlimited by old paradigms, including perceived boundaries and suffering. What vision are you building? What would you love to freely and beautifully contribute? In order to make freedom possible, I recommend you call upon a superpower you already possess: forgiveness. The very word "*for*-give" reminds us that giving is crucial to the process of personal healing and growth. Forgiveness is not about condoning injurious behaviors; it's about recognizing human frailty and releasing those involved from further entanglement. When you forgive, you both free yourself and embody compassion for all concerned.

It is possible to be both the forgiver and the forgiven. Often, when we come to examine the stories which have held us back on the creative path, we recognize that we need to forgive ourselves. That was certainly the case for me. I had to end my old self-blame for perceived shortcomings and decisions, for my former ignorance in not thinking *from* my dream early in adulthood. When I forgave myself, I could forgive others—even those who had passed from my life—and see anew how fortunate I've been to live a life with so many gifts. Forgiveness reconnects the forgiver with gratitude. Whom do you need to forgive, in your heart, for the experience of feeling damaged or held back? Make a list. Then create a ceremony, or simply compose and speak the needed lines and imagine being released. Once again, using your imagination with control is vital.

The act of forgiveness delivers healing power. You may do it to aid your personal growth, your unfettered creativity and your freedom to move forward. It's all right to forgive someone else for your own benefit; trust that your shift in attitude offers benefits for others, and don't deny them that. Don't be too proud to forgive; if you are, then you deny yourself the resulting healing and freedom that come of it. Remember the Buddhist adage that suffering is optional. So are freedom and joy.

Exercise 2: Revision

I offer the second exercise in a child's spirit, as it is quite playful, although it is challenging. Repeated over time, this activity strengthens your ability to control your thoughts, and it yields great benefits. It comes from the metaphysical teachings of Neville Goddard, and can be applied regardless of one's spiritual or materialist orientation. It's a practice he calls "The Pruning Shears of Revision." Done well, this mental activity raises your mood and point of attraction. Neville writes, "It is a most healthy and productive exercise to daily relive the day as you wish you had lived it, revising the scenes to make them conform to your ideals." He goes on to state, "Revision is of greatest importance when the motive is to change oneself, when there is a sincere desire to be something different, when the longing is to awaken the ideal active spirit of forgiveness." Use this technique when you desire to lift your spirits.

When living from your creative vision, attempting to see and feel your dream already manifest, the mental ability to revise your day keeps you moving forward in the direction of your fully realized dream, forgiving anyone whose behavior might otherwise have been viewed as an impediment to your progress. Neville explains that if, for example, you received a letter you didn't like today, review the day in your mind and use your imagination to see instead the letter you wish you had received. Here, I can readily add my own recent example. One day earlier this week, under deadline pressure to revise this chapter, I felt my writing process sabotaged by various unexpected, competing demands for my attention. By noon, despite all of my best intentions and mind training, I was in a funk. I was also a little sleep deprived and (ahem) hormonally challenged. When I stuck to my promise of meeting a friend for tea, I did so merely out of duty; I desperately wanted to get back to the writing, and I felt resentful and angry that my work time had been "taken" from me. The irony of feeling that way while revising a chapter on grace wasn't lost on me: I was frustrated by my emotional reaction. Suddenly, at the café, when I found myself staring into my friend's kind eyes, I found our meeting a *huge* relief and a blessing. My resentments vanished. I was very grateful for her companionship!

On the way home, I began to worry again about being behind on my project, and I wondered if I'd get enough done the next day. All at once I recalled how I could revise my day: I "remembered" my morning as though it had gone the way I'd intended. I saw myself meeting challenges smoothly as they arose, writing easily, contentedly, and well despite the interruptions. I cultivated the feeling of satisfaction that comes of being on track. In that moment, I had no doubt my next day's work would flow smoothly. At night, before falling asleep, once again I remembered my consistently harmonious, productive day. In the process, I also forgave myself for being so crabby and out of alignment earlier. I had compassion for my small self. As Goddard says, "To go forward to imagination is to forgive. Forgiveness is the life of the imagination. The art of living is the art of forgiving… every time one relives the event as it should have been lived, one is born again." As I write this, I've dialed up my mood to one of focused playfulness, and I've anticipated and already given thanks for my creatively fulfilling day.

I wish the same, or something greater still, for you.

Key Ideas

- You have the power to create the story of your experience.
- The ability to hold the thought you choose regardless of present circumstances is a powerful gift.
- By learning to see the good in your present situation, you can trust in possibilities that you still can't see from your present vantage point.
- You can shift from reacting to life's facts to responding to them thoughtfully and skilfully from your creative center.
- Repetition is the key to all learning and mastery.
- When employed repeatedly, the process of responding rather than reacting makes a breakthrough welcome.
- Change your view of the world and the world around you changes.
- When you can read your story as beautiful and grace-filled, regardless of the specific facts of the moment, you become a desirable beacon for others.
- In order for a new world to be created, the old one must be released. It takes courage to "die" into a new way of being.
- Things have a grace in the past when we recognize that experience is a powerful, supportive teacher.
- Consider "difficulties" as exercises in learning to use your powerful mind.
- In every story of self-recognition and transformation, a sense of connection to community and access to a power greater than one's own is crucial.
- Connecting with others whose expansive desires align with one's constructive, creative vision is paramount to moving forward.

- The terms "late" and "long" become unimportant in relation to the specifics of self-recognition and creative fulfillment.
- We often don't gain insight until we have a body of experience to look back on. Age is of no matter to the creative heart. We need to live in order to learn.
- Forgiveness frees us.
- When you're accountable to someone, your success skyrockets.
- Work with successful people. Be willing to invest in this, and be creative, not competitive. We grow by prospering one another.

Chapter 7
The Eagle:
Freeing Your Ability to Soar

To pray you open your whole self
To sky, to earth, to sun, to moon
To one whole voice that is you.
—Joy Harjo

Heaven is a state of mind.
—Raymond Holliwell

The Gift of Expectation

High expectation must match strong desire. It's not enough to wish to see something created and to visualize it, to use well-crafted affirmations, and even to do the work of taking action for your dream—excellent though it may be. I encourage you to identify your expectation level and begin to cultivate a sense of calm in knowing and fully expecting that the seeds you've sown will bear fruit. Practise seeing your intended results manifest in your mind before they manifest in reality. Focus your attention, work with passion, build your skills and your community and, above all, build your confidence. Build your faith in yourself, in whatever you conceive to be your creative source, and in the complete and perfect unfolding of your life.

On this point, I share with you a story from my long-ago acting days. At twenty-two, I found myself cast in an historical play penned by an earnest and very senior lady whose unflagging commitment to her craft was exemplary. As a fledgling artist with a thin skin, whenever the playwright's beseeching gaze fixed on me, I read it as a projection of disappointment. To offset a nagging feeling of falling short in her estimation, I consoled myself (as I was wont to do in those days) that the director liked my singing and had said I had "great hair." Unlike the union actors in the show, I was receiving no pay; my only reward was the hope of winning an audition and then being cast in the same director's summer comedy (an opportunity I eventually earned… and blew). I didn't recognize what a low level of expectation I had for my career, let alone see the inherent contradiction in working so hard yet expecting so little.

By day, I waitressed cheerily (albeit inexpertly), and by night, I performed in the play's first act. My character was a nervous, judgmental, and very pregnant young wife in a Madonna-blue dress, who died in childbirth several minutes before the intermission. The only other female character in the play faced a similarly bleak fate, succumbing to torture in the second act. While waiting for the curtain call, I relaxed in the kitchen backstage, playing cards, reading, and chatting happily with my new friend, Raphael, the sensitive and articulate custodian, who was Métis. A talk with him was always a bright spot in my day. Raphael had the name of a healing angel, and I found myself listening to stories of his initiation as a Native healer. Raphael gave me a gift I still cherish; now I'm glad to share his story with you.

In the wilds of western Canada, a spiritual teacher sent Raphael and a companion on a quest as part of their preparation for becoming healers. They were assigned to go into the woods along the shoreline and return with the feathers of an eagle. In Métis culture, as in many other Native traditions, the eagle is viewed as a mighty messenger to the Creator. The highest flyer of all living creatures, this great bird has the power to help us see beyond present circumstances. It also sits in the east on the medicine wheel, which in Métis society connotes leadership and courage. The eagle's feathers symbolize truth, power, and freedom: brown and white represent the Mother Earth from which our bodies come and to which they naturally return; dark and light represent a sacred balance. As two initiates on a quest to cultivate the vision and strength of character required for performing works of healing and transformation, Raphael and his companion were forbidden from disturbing nature's balance. A crucial condition of their quest was that they *do no harm* to the majestic animal—one that epitomizes strength and vision—in order to receive its feathers.

Raphael recalled for me how their expedition tested them on every level. For days they camped out in all weather, amidst the hungry blackflies and mosquitoes, surviving only on the fish they caught and the few dwindling supplies they'd brought with them. They hiked through the thick bush, keeping watch not only for eagle feathers, but for bears and cougars. Exposed to the elements, with no guarantee they'd fulfill their mission, the two remained in the wilderness, cut off from community, including those dear to them back home. When they were not keenly searching, or working arduously to survive, the men took time to sit in silence.

Here is a detail I wish to emphasize: "In silence," Raphael told me, "we waited." He didn't say they worried or discussed how they could cut their losses. He didn't say they dreaded the shame of going back empty handed. Were they afraid? At times, yes, of course. But their determination and courage outweighed their fear. They sat silently, upheld their vision, and prayed for guidance. At this point the expression "It was only a matter of time" does not adequately summarize what Raphael and his friend went through on their journey. It doesn't point to the physical, psychological, and spiritual challenges involved in searching the wilds for something that many would have argued wasn't worth the risk—something that might simply *never* appear.

One day, that "something" did appear, in the form of a dead eagle in their path. Having lived to maturity and died of natural causes, the magnificent creature became a gift for those men: the harvest of their initiatory cycle.

"We stayed with the bird a long time," said Raphael. "We spread its wings out in the sunlight on the shore and gave thanks. The eagle's feathers were a sign that we had passed our test."

The night after Raphael told me his story, I received something far more valuable than any paycheck I could have wished for from that production; it was by far my best gift from that short chapter of my life—apart from the young man's wise, steady, and gentle presence. When Raphael came to sweep the kitchen, he presented me with a feather from that eagle. Both the feather and my memory of that indelible moment still—almost thirty years later—fill me with a quiet sense of joy and awe. Back then, I had no idea what an honor it was to receive an item so sacred. I've had to grow in order to begin to appreciate Raphael's gift to me. During our last conversation, he said, "Keep it in your window for good health." And I have done so ever since.

For me, the eagle feather signifies an initiation story: one of learning the value not only of having the desire to complete a mission, but of having the belief and the faith that on some level the mission already *is* complete. Such rock-solid faith and confidence enable the quester to succeed. Raphael and his friend *knew* they'd find the eagle feathers; they just didn't know when, or where, or how. And they didn't need to. What's more, getting caught up in "how" likely would have blocked the manifestation from occurring. They acted on their inner guidance and belief, and they waited, taking time to sit in silence. Raphael's story of the eagle feathers is one of many that remind me of the creative process. The mighty bird is an emblem of gaining perspective and soaring from a place of higher vision. The men passed their test with hard work and focused determination; and equally important, they did so with a calm willingness to sit quietly. In silence came strength and clarity.

At the time of Raphael's fleeting presence in my life, I didn't fully comprehend the significance of the feather, in part because my creative life was rife with struggle. As it turned out, my own uncomfortable turning points related to increasing my awareness and accessing a broader vision: one of creative artistry, yes, and also of service. The eagle teaches us about milestones of service and leadership—and indeed, we are all leaders. Every one of us is charged with the mission to lead our own life, and to do it well. Back then, I couldn't see my way clearly, but I could put the feather in my window and know that, deep down, I was learning to read the signs.

This book has come to me like that feather—out of the air, and also from creativity's watery depths. It's the best kind of gift because it's not just for me; now it's yours, too.

The Eagle

The eagle is a bird associated with the Great Spirit across many cultures. In innumerable mythologies, the creature signifies communion with the heavens and divine power. But instead of recounting myriad eagle myths, I've chosen to share a poem by Native American poet Joy Harjo. Somehow this work connects me like no other with the great bird's presence.

Eagle Poem

To pray you open your whole self
To sky, to earth, to sun, to moon
To one whole voice that is you.
And know there is more
That you can't see, can't hear;
Can't know except in moments
Steadily growing, and in languages
That aren't always sound but other
Circles of motion.
Like eagle that Sunday morning
Over Salt River. Circled in blue sky
In wind, swept our hearts clean
With sacred wings.
We see you, see ourselves and know
That we must take the utmost care

> And kindness in all things.
> Breathe in, knowing we are made of
> All this, and breathe, knowing
> We are truly blessed because we
> Were born, and die soon within a
> True circle of motion,
> Like eagle rounding out the morning
> Inside us.
> We pray that it will be done
> In beauty.
> In beauty.

Harjo's poem reminds me that regardless of our age or circumstances, we can live our lives in beauty; I read her prayer as a calm, clear resolution.

The meaning of "in beauty" is open to each of us to interpret as we grow while seeking connection with, and guidance from, our higher nature. As we grow older, our eye for beauty can become much stronger and more discerning. The secret to keeping our vitality as we age is to keep looking and moving forward and to expect much. Growing older, we are given opportunities to develop greater awareness, empathy, and kindness. Life is about expansion, not contractive hardening. It's about "rounding out the morning," continuing to grow the whole way through adulthood until our last grateful breath. Daring to envision and follow through on our creative dreams, with a loving and generous heart, helps us grow in the best of ways.

The eagle soars and circles at a high altitude, and thus reminds us that a higher perspective is ever available. In order for us to gain access to a place of higher knowing, we must move, in the words of physicist and creativity specialist Amit Goswami, from the "outer arena" to the inner one. This meditative place can be a challenge to enter when the demands of life seem enormous, when the schedule is full and when one is tempted to push against the river instead of flowing with it. Yet in cultivating a practice of going inward, one also cultivates the conditions for creative confidence to grow and flourish. The inner state takes care of the outer. Meditating in the morning, taking breaks for sitting silently, for visualizing one's goals, for reflecting, for letting go and simply being—all this may feel counterintuitive when the book needs to be written, the calls made, the painting finished, the music composed and recorded, the dance choreographed and practiced and the day (or night) jobs done, not to mention the demands of family, travel time, chores. All these requirements, when combined, can put us into overdrive and cause anxiety. But they also give us all the more reason to let go on a daily basis and sit in silence. Goswami speaks of creativity as the artful process of alternating *being* and *doing*. In Bob Proctor's talks on human potential, he emphasizes that highly successful and productive people are relaxed; they take breaks.

For several years while I participated in a Zen Buddhist community, I cultivated a morning practice of meditating before journal writing. In the years following my formal involvement at the temple, I continued the practice of morning meditation. Then, for a while, as my life expanded with a beautiful new relationship (and ultimately marriage) to cultivate and a new household to share with our grown children, and as my teaching demands burgeoned, it felt like a challenge to make room for meditation. My partner Hugh and I attended retreats, and I did my best to find moments of calm mindfulness. Yet I missed sitting regularly. I wasn't even always aware of just how much.

Eventually, when I had the opportunity to write full-time at home in our empty nest, one would think I'd return easily to formal sitting each day and find time to access that higher perspective. Ironically, at home alone, finally able to prioritize my creative work, I pushed myself even more relentlessly. Once freed to avidly pursue my dream, I faced a challenging paradox: I had to learn to stop pursuing. Shifting from constantly *doing* to simply and routinely *being* can be scary for high-achiever types, because it's easy to feel that meditative time is "lost" time. Such fear of loss comes from scarcity thinking: worry that time will run out, that there won't be enough, that somehow if you don't push yourself you'll fall short. If you are tempted to think that way, give yourself a break and reflect. In truth, such time "out" is really crucial time "in."

When I realized what I'd temporarily lost in letting go of daily meditation, I also knew from experience that my access to a vast field of peace and strength could be regained. All I had to do was commit to changing a pattern. It's taken discipline to go from constantly pushing myself (an old, deeply ingrained habit) to incorporating daily times for simply sitting in awareness. Now, more than ever before, I take opportunities each day to consciously witness my mind and breath. The shift has led me to be more confident, relaxed and productive.

It is when I don't feel like meditating, going for a meditative walk or practicing yoga (a great interplay of being and doing) that I know I'd most benefit from one or more of those activities. Stephen Farmer takes the eagle's point of view in his *Power Animals* chapter on the great bird's gifts: "When your vision is too narrow, and you can't find solutions, take a look from where I see.... You must have the courage to relinquish stale and comfortable habits and soar into unknown realms and new realities, continually expanding your view." Ironically, for me, the stale and comfortable habit was one of driving myself to action in what I thought was service to my dream. What I needed, however, was to let go, to sit, to take breaks, to work out, to take walks—to give myself sacred time out, on a daily basis, so the old paradigm of overwork (and its attendant feeling of desperation) could be transcended.

Working harder is not the same as working smarter. This idea can seem like heresy to a driven creator. But greater perception comes from switching to a different energy level than the hard-driving mode that seems to be the current default in our culture. A wise creator knows the value of stillness and silence. Consider Thomas Edison, a brilliant creative in the field of applied science, a man who was granted 2,332 patents. When he needed to find answers, he took a break from pushing himself and journeyed to "the land of the solution," which for Edison meant entering a deeply relaxed state in his rocking chair. That calm time out (and in) routinely yielded new ideas, including, often, the very answers he was seeking. For peace and inspiration, writer Gertrude Stein went out each day and found a place to sit and gaze upon cows in the fields. Like other creative geniuses, Ludwig van Beethoven accessed ideas and found rejuvenation in daily walking.

Countless artists meditate, and for good reason. Contemporary film director and painter David Lynch has written a book about the vital connections between meditation and creativity. In *Catching the Big Fish: Meditation, Consciousness and Creativity*, Lynch recounts his experience of discovering transcendental meditation in 1973, and of remaining a steadfast practitioner ever since. He ardently recommends meditation as a way of accessing creative flow and fresh ideas. Lynch writes, "Personally, I think intuition can be sharpened and expanded through meditation, diving into the Self. There's an ocean of consciousness inside each of us, and it's an ocean of solutions. When you dive into that ocean, that consciousness, you enliven it." Lynch describes meditation as the perfect practice for coping with the stresses inherent in pursuing a career in the arts—the film business in particular. Through a daily routine of sitting in silence, he explains, "transcending makes life more like a game—a fantastic game. And creativity can really flow." At first, letting go into conscious being instead of doing may seem counterintuitive, yet it's in the periods of our most creatively demanding, intense work that we can benefit most from quiet sitting. Lynch points out that he normally meditates in the morning and evening—unless he's directing a film, in which case he meditates more.

The eagle is associated with mystical power, and for me it is a reminder to sit quietly each day and transcend—perhaps even when I feel most compelled by my to-do list. The feather remains in the window of my study, where I keep my meditation cushion. In going deep within the inner arena, we have the possibility of accessing what Goswami calls the "quantum self." Art is a series of problems to solve. We can't force creative solutions—flashes of insight, inspirations, glimpses of next steps—but we can learn to make them welcome. The eagle serves as an emblem of working smarter, not harder. As it soars to great heights, surveying its territory while easily riding the thermals, it flows with life rather than pushing. It conserves energy.

Quantum Leaping

Solutions and flashes of insight may not come during times of quiet sitting, of riding the steady thermals of the breath, and of emptying oneself of stress to simply watch one's thoughts. Lynch points out that for him such flashes usually come *after* meditating. I find that sometimes ideas come to me both during and after the process, but more often after—sometimes at the oddest moments, and always when I'm relaxed. Goswami cites many examples of "discontinuity" in creativity—that is, instances of important ideas showing up when the creative thinker is not in the regular work context: either busy at something mundane or out of the daily routine completely. "Creative thoughts that shift our contexts or reveal new meaning are discontinuous leaps from our ordinary stream-of-consciousness thoughts," writes Goswami. I return to Lynch's idea about daily meditation enabling the practitioner to approach life as a game, and I celebrate the playfulness in that perspective. The more we can learn to trust that the answers and ideas we seek already exist and are available to us, the more we can let go and simply watch and listen. Then we may find that ideas suddenly rush to us while we are at the gym, making lunch, raking the yard, washing dishes, driving to work, walking to the store or the café, etc.

When those ideas come, they often arrive in what Goswami characterizes as a "quantum leap" of creativity. In his book *Quantum Creativity*, he cites various examples of mathematicians and composers discovering entire solutions and future compositions in one fell swoop. A poem may come not in phrases and lines but in whole stanzas. "This wholeness is characteristic of the quantum nature of creative insights, and even when an idea is only part of a whole solution, it acts as a seed for the wholeness that follows."

The shift in awareness that occurs when we take a break corresponds with literal shifts in brain-wave frequency. Years ago, I was fortunate to discover the work of Bill Harris at the Centerpointe Research Institute, and to learn to use binaural beats, a form of brain entrainment, in order to induce the brain to shift from its usual beta (rapid, waking-state) wave pattern to an alpha or even theta wave pattern. In *Thresholds of the Mind*, Harris writes that the theta wave state "is associated with enhanced creativity, memory, healing and integrative experiences, where we put together previously disparate pieces of information, leading to an 'ah-ha' experience of sudden understanding." Using technology such as Harris's Holosync series, or other binaural beat recordings (which are often embedded in relaxation music today), it's possible for a meditator to enter more tranquil and expansive brain wave states fairly readily. While I'm not a scientist in a position to formally recommend such audio programs, I can tell you I've been using Centerpointe recordings for years, in addition to routinely sitting in silence. I've felt the benefits of brain entrainment, not the least of which has been an experience of increased calm, focus, and confidence.

Conserving energy, resting, sitting, being—all of these states lead to the frequency of calm confidence. When on that frequency, we learn to recognize and grasp solutions as they arise. As we learn to ride the thermals each day, to live and work efficiently, we create mental space and time for soaring and diving. The eagle is a bird of great vision. In fact, the eagle's vision is eight times greater than human sight. (It has to be—some eagles fly as high as 10,000 feet.) Taking time out, while trusting your vision of the outcome—of the "what" and not the "how"—invites new ideas.

To the person who takes the time to welcome them, solutions come in many ways. They may be in the form of artistic inspiration, or they may be other people—have you ever noticed how sometimes individuals come into your life right at the time you need the particular skills or gifts that they have? They can also arrive more mysteriously. Meditation can help you allow for the possibility that help is *already right here,* even if not apparent from your present vantage point. Stay open to the possibility of aid from forces you can't see. Trust in Emerson's adage that "Once you make a decision, the whole universe conspires to make it happen." Likewise, recall the words of Shakespeare's Hamlet: "There are more things in heaven and earth, Horatio, / Than are dreamt of in your philosophy." Heaven is here among us if we will only open ourselves to it.

Detachment

In the creative process, another leap, inextricable from the quantum, is the leap of faith. What happens when we finish the project we've been working on and we send it into the world? How do we do so with detachment? Remember, the eagle soars—she doesn't flap around worried about things not turning out. She flies patiently, confidently.

You can learn to be this way in your creative life. Remember that your most successful work is that which brings value to others. This is such a fundamental idea. Our creative work is a form of service. I choose to believe that inspired creation comes from Spirit, and it goes to Spirit. Substitute other language if you like: call it the unified field; call it oneness. Trust that whatever is greater than you, and also in you, gave to you the burning desire to see your work realized. Once you've done all that you can do to see your work through to completion, hold your creation lightly; Mary Morrissey says, "Hold your dream with an open palm." You can say, "This, or something greater still." You can uphold your high expectation while maintaining calm faith, confidence, and detachment. In twelve-step work, a key step (number three) is turning experience over to a higher power. If you have honed your skills and done your very best, then trust your creative source to guide the rest of the process—even when that process appears rocky. As I stated earlier, let go of the "how" once the process is out of your hands. Just as grown children have their own lives and ultimately fly free, so too does your work. Your growth is truly your most important achievement, and you can ensure that it happens regardless of the end results of any creative project. Growth is what keeps us young. Release the urge to worry and control. Move forward and trust that everything's unfolding rightly.

Once, when I asked Bob Proctor what it feels like to hold a vision both confidently and with detachment, he reminded me that in truth we own nothing in this world. We are, each one of us, custodians. We can care for things and enjoy things while we're here; and one day, ultimately, we must be prepared to let them go. Be confident, and also trust that whatever you create from your beautiful heart and mind finds its place and serves its purpose. We don't *own* anything, including either the process or the outcome—but we can *enjoy* all of it.

In *Animal Speak*, Ted Andrews describes the mating ritual of the bald eagle. I love his description, as it points to living passionately and on purpose:

> A powerful form of sky dancing occurs. The birds soar, loop, and plunge into "deep dives." At a certain point they grab each other's feet and lock talons, rolling and falling, until the mating ritual is completed. Then they separate and soar upwards to repeat the process over and over again.

For the eagle, as for us, risk and trust are inextricable from the creative process. So often our work requires free fall. This is the creative life! If you find yourself worrying about the results of one creation, be sure to soar upward and create again.

The best move I could have made at the end of my first experience of writing, revising and completing a novel was to start another book—this book, in fact. And after this, I'll write another. All of life can be a process of artful soaring and falling, doing and being.

Trust your wings while they're yours to fly with. And when the time comes, trust that you can let them go, too.

**Claiming The Eagle's Gift:
Soaring with Perspective**

Exercise 1: Raise Your Altitude through Study

In order to function at a high level, we can routinely put our minds in alignment with such positive, inspirational and constructive ideas that our creative lives become ever more expansive. To do this, it is advisable not only to meditate, journal and read uplifting works, but to commit to daily study. That means fifteen to twenty minutes of daily review and reinforcement. Repetition is the key to building your skills, and it's also the best way to install new and beneficial patterns of thought.

I encourage you to have a look at the bibliography included at the end of this book—and bear in mind that I have only scratched the surface of the great material that's out there. In seeking to move ideas from "out there" to "in here"—i.e., into your new, expansive, and life-affirming paradigm, you can adopt the habit of rereading the books that inspire you to take constructive action. Find writers whose work you love and reread their most instructive chapters slowly, reflectively and repeatedly over a long period with the intent to grow from the experience. (I often commit to reading a key chapter daily for ninety days.) Invite their breakthroughs to become your own.

Exercise 2: Raise Your Strength through Listening

Increasingly, I've come to value Robert Collier's forthright words of advice: "You know the strength of a chain doesn't lie in its strongest link, no matter how strong, but in its weakest. Find your weak link, and then strengthen it." As discussed at the end of Chapter 2 ("The Flicker"), listening to uplifting recordings can dramatically help you to shift to a higher perspective, allowing for new insights, advice, and ways of being to come sharply into view. If you're experiencing a feeling of weakness in an area of your life (and who isn't?), find motivational and instructive recordings in that area and listen to them daily in order to consciously build your knowledge, strength, and skills. For example, if you are a highly creative being with gifts for this world, yet you struggle to figure out how to finance your creative life, seek out useful recordings on increasing wealth; make learning to master money a part of your daily routine. Commit to growing in whatever area needs attention right now. Stay open to the ideas that drop into your awareness. Learn to turn up the volume on the areas that need attention until, by actively listening, you turn them into strengths.

Exercise 3: Explore Guided Imagery for Motivation

The guided imagery script that follows was inspired by my work with Master Coach Derrick Sweet, another wise and generous teacher whose presence has touched my life. It's intended for you to read aloud and record in a slow, soft and rhythmic voice. The script is designed to help you create an expansive, motivational experience. You may choose to run a quiet music track behind your reading, but you don't need to. As you read, and later when you listen to your recording in a relaxed, alpha-wave state, you'll be prompted to bring forth positive ideas as you nurture your own creative growth and vision. Feel free to pause where you'd like to in the reading, and to adjust any of the words to suit your particular desires. Of course, you may wish to create another script entirely, using a different metaphorical focus. Go for it. The sky's the limit!

If orally reading and recording the script are too much for you to do right now, earmark the page and schedule to return to it later, when you're ready to experiment and dream. (A recording is included in the audio version of this book. You can also find it, along with other motivational recordings, on my website at www.robinblackburnmcbride.com.)

Listen to this script while sitting comfortably or lying down. (**Note:** Do not listen to imagery recordings while driving or operating machinery.)

Here we go.

Lucid Dream Script: Transformations

In this experience, you are in a dream state, and you know that you are dreaming. When you find yourself experiencing new abilities in new settings, and moving in ways you normally don't in your human life, you accept your situation because you can control your actions in the dream state. You are comfortable, safe, relaxed, and in charge of your actions and responses.

Curled in a ball, you feel all the security of a closed, snug world. You're breathing calmly now, and you are warm. You've been this way a long time, you realize, and you notice that your world isn't changing. It continues to be dark, and for the first time you realize it's hard to move in this world. Each time you shift a little, you meet resistance. The more you push at the hard shell, the more limiting it seems, and the more longing you feel to stretch — until all you yearn for is to reach beyond the old boundaries, because you've been tightly curled for so long...

So long in a familiar, narrow space that once served you and even nourished you, and now must be released. You are ready to let it go...

Finally, you stretch your limbs and hear a crack — then another. And suddenly: light. It's so bright that you squint, while your eyes adjust, and you realize you've never had to see so clearly before. As you continue to shift, every cell in your body feels relief in extending past the old limits.

And the shell falls away.

Here you are, all at once, in a nest atop a high building where the air feels cool. You glimpse more buildings around you, shiver a little in the breeze, and snuggle down among the soft materials of your newly discovered home. Days go by, and you are nourished here in these cozy confines which become your new source of warmth and shelter against the elements. Yet despite the comfort of this nest, often you look beyond its carefully woven boundaries and feel desire — a sense of longing to use your growing limbs and abilities, to move in ways you know you'll need to if you're ever to go beyond these walls. Each day, you feel larger and stronger. You feel the feathers filling in your wings now, and you dream of spreading those new wings and gliding in the air as you see other birds doing. You close your eyes and visualize yourself gliding. It scares you a little; but your desire is greater than your fear.

It takes energy for you to grow each day, and you know you're moving forward. While your circumstances haven't changed yet, your mind prepares a flight path...

One day you're suddenly lifted above the limits of your old home. The wind whistles, and it thrills you, and you're afraid that you're not ready...

Now you're moving through the air! And this doesn't feel like gliding — it feels like falling! Yet as you take a deep breath and concentrate on what you've dreamed of — flight — you find that your wings beat automatically; how easily they do the work they were meant to do.

As you near the ground at a much slower rate, you realize that you're not falling. Your eyes are keen to read this new world, and you spy words written in bright pink letters on the sidewalk. A child's been here, and spelled out every positive emotion in chalk. You survey the words as you flutter a little awkwardly above them, and you ask yourself which emotion you'd like to land on. Which one would serve you best right now? Take a moment to consider. Know that you can change your mind just by imagining a fresh, new chalk word, any time — and choose. [Pause.] *As you touch down for a moment, notice that some of the bright pink chalk rubs off upon your feet and tail feathers. Your chosen feeling gives you lift.*

You're in the air again. Only this time, you fly better. There's much to navigate: all the city streets, the different heights of things, all the people, cars and bicycles in motion, all the posts, poles, mailboxes and buildings. The buses, too. And the other birds! Oh, how you wish you could rise up to the chattering sparrows and starlings, and up again, higher still, to the cawing crows — and to those seagulls! As they call and wheel far above you, each bird seems perfect in its flight. Concentrating on the brightness of your chosen emotion, you rise a little higher, to the level of the second-storey windows where people stand and stare. But you don't think about them now, because you're flying — flying! — straight ahead, adjusting your course as you need to.

And you realize you can fly for miles.

You also recognize that you've achieved your dream of flight. It came naturally. Now it's time to choose another dream, and something wonderful draws you. You fix your attention on moving beyond the city limits, to your new vision: trees. You don't want just a few, but many. Each time you pass a city park full of trees, you yearn to find more of them. And even though you've never seen a forest before, you know one must exist because you've seen it in your mind. Desiring tall trees, and borne aloft on your feeling and your new dream, you continue until you reach the city limit and gaze upon a whole new landscape. Sure enough, in the distance, your eyes spy a densely wooded hill beyond the fields. As you near the steep, forested slope, you exalt in the feeling of having found what you were looking for, and as you do, you see something unexpected. Up on the very top of the hill is one tree that's strikingly different from the rest.

Beating your wings with great force, you ascend. On the tallest tulip tree are long strips of white cloth tied to branches. A child's been here, and written positive beliefs in spring-green letters. So many! Which belief will you choose? Higher and higher you must fly to reach the strip that's yours. Take a moment to search for the belief that serves you best right now, and find it tied to the top bough of the towering tulip tree. There it is. [Pause.] *Know that anytime in your imagination you can come back to choose another. When you rise up to that belief, you discover a place to rest. Here, on the highest point of the highest tree on the hill, you see the tiny, twinkling city far behind you, and the softly darkening fields as you sit in silence for a while...*

In the dawn light, your chosen belief gives you lift. Higher still, and ever forward, you fly beyond the forested hill. Your next dream is to reach the faraway mountains you see faintly, in the distance. With your empowering belief comes new energy, and you're a master glider now — beating your great wings intermittently, and those mountains seem pulled to you, as much as you are pulled to them. They grow larger as you discover you're a magnet for your dream. And you keep flying. When you need to swoop down for nourishment, you do, as your wings continue growing, pulsing smoothly, and you are learning beautifully how to use your gifts.

You and the mountains are very close now, almost touching. As you ascend again, looking for the best ledge to land on, you're suddenly drawn to a sheer rock wall of carvings. A child's been here, and inscribed many positive thoughts — enough to fill the entire surface. Wheeling in circles, you search for the thought you'd love right now. Which thought gives you life? Take a moment to decide. [Pause.] Know that in your mind you can return any time and choose another... Now see your chosen thought carved at the very top where a cedar root juts out through the rock face and welcomes you: the perfect place to land and sit in silence for a while.

You realize that you are far beyond where you'd imagined you could fly. Recalling your desired emotion, your empowering belief and your chosen thought, you reflect for a long time, gazing out at a vast world you'd once only imagined. You're at home here on this perch, and soon, you're in the company of other eagles on this mountain. In fact, you realize they've been around you all along.

Together, you weave an aerie on the thought that gives you life, knowing here is your place to dream.

Then your eyes spy something far above and beyond, and you fly toward it. A child's been here, and left white letters in the sky. Expectations. Which one lifts you higher? Choose a positive expectation. [Pause.] Know that any time you can return and choose another.

Take a moment simply to feel the wonder of this altitude and to know that anytime in your mind it's yours. Now your lucid dream of being an eagle is coming to an end — for the time being. As you rise to your chosen expectation, take a moment to play and soar, and do a few loops. Know your eagle spirit is about to transform back into your human form. Up among the highest expectations, find a thermal and ride it easily and effortlessly, *far across the sky to the very place you choose to start from now in your human form. As you awaken from this journey, a Forever Child with many gifts, know that somehow the dreaming eagle is a part of you. You've flown together through dreams before, and you will again. Feel relief in every cell of your arms and legs as they stretch. Note the emotion, belief, thought and expectation you choose for yourself right now in your journey. What is your creative dream? Expect it. For a few minutes, fully visualize it and feel it as already manifest. Know that it is already yours.*

Key Ideas

- In manifesting creative dreams, match your expectations to your desires.
- Calmly and confidently expect the seeds you've sown to bear fruit.
- Building faith leads to building confidence.
- In trusting a creative vision, let go of the "how" and concentrate on the "what."
- Take time each day to sit in silence.
- In cultivating a practice of going inward, you also cultivate the conditions for creative confidence to grow.
- Creativity is a process of alternately being and doing.
- At our busiest, we can benefit most from meditating three times per day.
- "Highly successful people are relaxed. They take breaks." —Bob Proctor
- Working harder is not the same as working smarter.
- Trust in the help of forces you can't see.
- We are custodians; we own nothing. And we can care for, contribute, and enjoy so much while we are here.
- Study works that give you life.

- Strengthen what's been weak in you up until now, so that from this moment forward you become stronger.
- Take time to recognize and cherish your own growth.

Postscript

Robin Blackburn McBride's debut novel, *The Shining Fragments*, will be published by Guernica Editions in 2018.

Acknowledgments

No book comes alone into the world through a single person. This one came in a dark hour giving way to light, and in countless, indelible moments of human connection.

Thanks to Mary Morrissey for arriving in my life at the perfect time to show me grace and a brave new world. You are a teacher's teacher, and a forever-friend of my heart. I am deeply grateful to you, and to your exemplary team and community.

Thanks to Marie Forleo for opening my eyes to possibilities and encouraging me to put writing and coaching together "under one roof." At the time we were discussing my website, but your response caused me to think about so much more.

Thanks to Bob Proctor for sharing wisdom so generously, and for showing up on a personal call that changed my life.

Thanks to Peggy McColl for convincing me these birds were a book, not a daydream. You are a writer's friend and guide. I am inspired by the change-makers you draw to your circles of support, and by the knowledge and care you extend so brilliantly.

Thanks to the groups of fellow writers I've been privileged to be a part of. I have loved our heart-centered mastermind calls, our communions.

Thanks to my cherished accountability partners, Life Mastery Consultants Lynn Tranchell and Julie Jones Hamilton, for believing in me. May I be a mirror to your light.

Thanks to the wonderful artists who have contributed directly to this book: writer Julie Roorda, for being *Birdlight*'s first reader and discerning editor, and a good friend; Elizabeth d'Anjou, for picking up the torch so expertly at the copy-editing stage; Amy Brown for your vigilant proofreading; Chum McLeod for your magical drawings; Patti Knoles for the beautiful *Birdlight* cover; and Katie McBride for music and sound production on the audio version.

Thanks to the professionals who helped me bring this book into form and connect with readers: Carolyn Flower and Steve Walters at Flower Communications for design and promotional assistance; Daveed Flexer, Laura K Beauparlant, Amy Wong, and my daughter

Charlotte Klein for help with social media; dream-builders Damon Darnell and Cliff Pelloni at Efluential Publishing for specialized guidance, publicity, and launch planning.

Thanks to the many writers, artists, and thought leaders whose messages have uplifted me and found their way onto these pages, carrying this project forward.

Finally, thanks to my dear husband Hugh, my soul's partner in creativity, and to my family for your love and support.

We are one story.

Sources

I would like to thank the authors and copyright holders for permission to use the following material:

Andrews, Ted. *Animal Speak: The Spiritual & Magical Powers of Creatures Great & Small*, by Ted Andrews. Woodbury, MN: Llewellyn Publications, 1993. Excerpts and paraphrases used with with permission.

Campbell, Joseph. "You enter the forest..." From *A Joseph Campbell Companion*, edited by Diane K. Osbon. New York: HarperPerennial, 1991. Reprinted with permission.

Harjo, Joy. "Eagle Poem" from *In Mad Love and War* © 1990 by Joy Harjo. Reprinted with permission of Wesleyan University Press.

Hillman, James. *The Soul's Code: In Search of Character and Calling*. New York: Random House, 1996. Excerpt used with permission.

Kavanagh, Patrick. "Ploughman." From *Selected Poems*, edited by Antoinette Quinn, 2nd edition. London: Penguin, 2000. Reprinted with permission.

Reid, Bill, and Bringhurst, Robert. "Raven and the First Men." From *The Raven Steals the Light,* 2nd edition. Madeira Park, BC: Douglas & McIntyre, 1996. Reproduced with permission.

A Way of Being Free, copyright 1997. Reprinted by kind permission of Ben Okri.

Thanks also to Prill Boyle for her kindness in response to my inquiry about *Defying Gravity: A Celebration of Late-Blooming Women*. Cincinnati: Clerissy Press, 2005.

Bibliography

Chapter 1

The Owl: Freeing Your Courage

Andrews, Ted. *Animal Speak: The Spiritual & Magical Powers of Creatures Great & Small*. Woodbury, MN: Llewellyn Publications, 1993.

Campbell, Joseph. *A Joseph Campbell Companion*. Edited by Diane K. Osbon. New York: HarperPerennial, 1991.

Grimm, Jacob and Wilhelm. *Grimm's Complete Fairy Tales*. Nelson Doubleday Inc., 1954. (Originally published 1857.)

Kelley, David. "How to Build Your Creative Confidence." TED.com. TED Conferences, March 2012. Retrieved from www.ted.com/talks/david_kelley_how_to_build_your_creative_confidence?language=en

Robertson, Ian H. *The Winner Effect: The Neuroscience of Success and Failure*. New York: St. Martin's Press, 2012.

Rumi. *The Essential Rumi*. Translated by Coleman Barks. New York: HarperOne, 2004.

Chapter 2

The Flicker: Freeing Your Trust and Confidence

Andrews, Ted. *Animal Speak.*—See Chapter 1.

Cameron, Julia. *The Artist's Way: A Spiritual Path to Higher Creativity*. New York: Jeremy P. Tarcher/Putnum, 1992.

Goldberg, Natalie. *Writing Down the Bones: Freeing the Writer Within*. Boston: Shambala, 1986.

Hill, Napoleon. *Think and Grow Rich*. New York: Jeremy P. Tarcher/Penguin, 2005. (Originally published 1937.)

Sher, Gail. *One Continuous Mistake: Four Noble Truths for Writers*. New York: Penguin Compass, 1999.

Tate, Peter. *Flights of Fancy: Birds in Myth, Legend and Superstition*. London: Random House, 2007.

Chapter 3

The Robin: Freeing Your Authenticity

Andreasen, Nancy. "Secrets of the Creative Brain." *The Atlantic*. July/August, 2014. Retrieved from http://www.theatlantic.com/magazine/archive/2014/07/secrets-of-the-creative-brain/372299/

Andrews, Ted. *Animal Speak*.—See Chapter 1.

Angelou, Maya. Interview with Krista Tippett. "Maya Angelou on Courage." *On Being*. Tuesday, July 8, 2014. Web. Retrieved from http://www.onbeing.org/blog/maya-angelou-on-courage/6480

Campbell, Joseph. *A Joseph Campbell Companion*.—See Chapter 1.

Clark, Glenn. *The Man Who Tapped the Secrets of the Universe*. Swannanoa, NC: Kessinger Publishing, 2006. Print. (Originally published 1946.)

Emerson, Ralph Waldo. "Self-Reliance." *The Spiritual Emerson*. New York: Jeremy P. Tarcher/Penguin, 2008.

Goddard, Neville. *The Power of Awareness. Awakened Imagination*. New York: Jeremy P. Tarcher/Penguin, 2012. (Originally published 1952.)

Hendricks, Gay. *The Big Leap: Conquer Your Hidden Fear and Take Life to the Next Level*. New York: HarperCollins, 2009.

Hillman, James. *The Soul's Code: In Search of Character and Calling*. New York: Random House, 1996.

Jobs, Steve. "How to Live Before You Die." TED.com. Stanford University Commencement Speech, June 2005. Retrieved from https://www.ted.com/talks/steve_jobs_how_to_live_before_you_die

Tate, Peter. *Flights of Fancy*.—See Chapter 2.

Chapter 4

The Crow and the Raven: Freeing Your Vision, Intuition, and Action

Savage, Candace. *Bird Brains: The Intelligence of Crows, Ravens, Magpies and Jays*. Vancouver: Greystone Books of Douglas & McIntyre, 1995.

Feher-Elston, Catherine. *Ravensong: A Natural and Fabulous History of Ravens and Crows*. New York: Jeremy P. Tarcher/Penguin, 2005.

Andrews, Ted. *Animal Speak*.—See Chapter 1.

Goldberg, Natalie. *Writing Down the Bones.*—See Chapter 2.

Hill, Napoleon. *Think and Grow Rich.*—See Chapter 2.

Kavanagh, Patrick. "Ploughman." *Selected Poems.* Edited by Antoinette Quinn. 2nd edition. London: Penguin, 2000.

Reid, Bill, and Bringhurst, Robert. "Raven and the First Men." *The Raven Steals the Light.* 2nd edition. Madeira Park, BC: Douglas & McIntyre, 1996.

Chapter 5

The Duck: Freeing Your Emotions and Discernment

Andersen, Hans Christian. "The Ugly Duckling." *Classics of Children's Literature.* Ed. Giffith, John W. and Frey, Charles H. 3rd ed. New York: MacMillan, 1992. Print. (Originally published 1843.)

Bettelheim, Bruno. *The Uses of Enchantment: The Meaning and Importance of Fairy Tales.* 3rd edition. New York: Vintage, 2010. (Originally published 1976.)

Brown, Brené. *The Gifts of Imperfection.* Center City, MN: Hazelden, 2010.

Cameron, Julia. *The Right to Write: An Invitation and Initiation into the Writing Life.* New York: Jeremy P. Tarcher/Putnam, 1998.

Csikszentmihalyi, Mihaly. *Flow: The Psychology of Optimal Experience.* New York: Harper Perennial Modern Classics, 2008. (Originally published 1990.)

Frost, Robert. Interview with Richard Poirier. "The Art of Poetry No. 2." *The Paris Review: No. 24.* Summer-Fall 1960. Retrieved from http://www.theparisreview.org/interviews/4678/the-art-of-poetry-no-2-robert-frost

Halifax, Joan. *The Fruitful Darkness: A Journey Through Buddhist Practice and Tribal Wisdom.* New York: Grove Press, 1993.

Hay, Louise. *You Can Heal Your Life.* Carlsbad, CA: Hay House, 1999.

Ibsen, Henrik. *The Wild Duck.* Translated by Anonymous. Mineola, NY: Dover Publications, Inc., 2000. (Originally published 1884.)

Jung, C. G. *Memories, Dreams, Reflections.* Ed. Aniela Jaffe. Trans. Richard and Clara Winston. Revised ed. New York: Vintage, 1989. (Originally published 1963.)

Chapter 6

The Swan: Freeing Recognition

Andersen, Hans Christian. "The Ugly Duckling." – See Chapter 5.

Andrews, Ted. *Animal Speak.* – See Chapter 1.

Boyle, Prill. *Defying Gravity: A Celebration of Late-Blooming Women.* Cincinnati: Clerissy Press, 2005. Print.

Cash, Rosanne. Interview with Krista Tippett. "Rosanne Cash – Time Traveler." *On Being.* June 5, 2014. Retrieved from http://www.onbeing.org/program/rosanne-cash-time-traveler/transcript/6343

Collier, Robert. *The Secret of the Ages.* 3rd edition. New York: Jeremy P. Tarcher/Penguin, 2007. (Originally published under this title 1926.)

Emerson, Ralph Waldo. "Spiritual Laws." *The Spiritual Emerson.* New York: Jeremy P. Tarcher/Penguin, 2008.

Farmer, Stephen D. *Power Animals: How to Connect with Your Animal Spirit Guide.* Carlsbad: Hay House, 2004.

Goddard, Neville. *The Power of Awareness.* – See Chapter 3.

Halifax, Joan. *The Fruitful Darkness.* – See Chapter 5.

Nhat Hanh, Thich. *The Heart of the Buddha's Teaching: Transforming Suffering into Peace, Joy, and Liberation.* New York: Broadwy Books, 1999. Print.

Okri, Ben. *A Way of Being Free.* 2nd edition. London: Phoenix, 2002.

Williamson, Marianne. *A Return to Love: Reflections on the Principles of A Course in Miracles.* New York: HarperCollins, 1993.

Chapter 7

The Eagle: Freeing Your Ability to Soar

Andrews, Ted. *Animal Speak.* – See Chapter 1.

Farmer, Stephen D. *Power Animals.* — See Chapter 6.

Goswami, Amit. *Quantum Creativity: Think Quantum, Be Creative.* Carlsbad: Hay House, 2014.

Harjo, Joy. "Eagle Poem." *Mad Love and War.* Hanover, PA: Wesleyan University Press, 1990.

Harris, Bill. *Thresholds of the Mind: Your Personal Roadmap to Success, Happiness, and Contentment*. Beaverton: Centerpointe Press, 2007.

Holliwell, Raymond. *Working with the Law: 11 Truth Principles for Successful Living*. 5th edition. Camarillo, CA: DeVorss, 2012.

Lynch, David. *Catching the Big Fish: Meditation, Consciousness, and Creativity*. New York: Jeremy P. Tarcher/Penguin, 2007.

Meet Robin

One of Robin Blackburn McBride's great joys in life is helping individuals of all ages find their true passion—and then bring out, develop, and apply their innate creative gifts to living a life they love, centered on that passion. To help them bridge the gap between their present circumstances and the realization of their vision ... to feel fulfilled, confident, more productive, and balanced in and between all areas of their life.

Born to a family of avid readers, teachers, musicians, artists, and storytellers in mid-sixties Toronto, Robin's love of the arts—and of creativity in all its myriad forms—came naturally. Over the years, she has built up a varied multidisciplinary arts background, with experience in visual art (drawing, painting, collage), music (singing, musical theatre, violin), and theatre (as an actress).

After majoring in drama at the University of Toronto (with additional degrees in English and Education), Robin worked for a time as a professional actress. But it was during her twenty years of teaching at one of Canada's premier private schools that she discovered perhaps her greatest gift, and deepest love: fostering creativity in others.

Because of her insatiable commitment to lifelong learning, Robin has trained extensively with some of the best in the field, including Mary Morrissey, Bob Proctor, Peggy McColl, Marie Forleo, and Derrick Sweet.

Her experiences with these mentors, coupled with her arts and teaching careers, are what naturally led Robin to becoming such a sought-after Transformational Coach, specializing in dream building and creativity. Having found success following her own passion, Robin now dedicates herself to helping others live creative, vision-centered lives.

My Heartfelt Wish for You...

I hope you've enjoyed *Birdlight* and the time we've spent together here.

And I sincerely hope you'll put what you've learned (and the inspiration you've gleaned) to good use in bringing about whatever marvellous changes and creations your heart holds dear.

Let's not allow our relationship to end here, though.

Instead, *join me online* for even more resources to help enhance your creativity. There's always something new – whether it's on my blog or in the next book (like the *Birdlight* sequel) or audio release. Check out my webinar training series. (That one is just now getting off the ground, and there are B-I-G plans for the near future!)

My website is also the place to go when you want to contact me with any questions or suggestions for books or blog posts you'd like to see, and to enquire about attending or hosting one of my talks or workshops (private or public). You can also purchase additional products in the *Birdlight* line on the site.

You'll see that I also offer a full range of transformational coaching options, including Mary Morrissey's *Life Mastery Institute* programs.

There are **FREE gifts** set aside for you, too, just waiting for you to drop by and claim them – such as the downloadable **Birdlight** audio visualization session.

And while you're there, be sure to register for **FREE** e-mail updates so you'll always know when I publish anything new. I also send occasional tips and strategies for further enhancing your creative spirit. I wouldn't want you to miss out.

Once again, let me say how much I appreciate this chance to share with you, and to contribute to your journey to a more creatively fulfilling life – one that is lived the way you dream of living!

Now use the link below to visit my website so we can keep the conversation going. I'll be waiting for you there.

www.robinblackburnmcbride.com

www.ingramcontent.com/pod-product-compliance
Lightning Source LLC
LaVergne TN
LVHW051600070426
835507LV00021B/2683